HIGHDAYS
&
HOLIDAYS

by

FLORENCE A

and

ELIZABETH McCARRICK

DECORATED BY EMMA L. BROCK

E. P. DUTTON & CO., INC.
NEW YORK

AMERICAN BOOK—STRATFORD PRESS, INC., NEW YORK
SBN 0-525-31962-x

Acknowledgments

For permission to use copyrighted material included in this volume, the compilers are indebted to the following authors and publishers:

D. APPLETON & COMPANY—for "Robert of Lincoln" and "Twenty-second of February," from *Poetical Works of William Cullen Bryant.*

ATLANTA CONSTITUTION—for "Old Flag Forever," by Frank Stanton.

THE ATLANTIC MONTHLY and the respective authors—for "Taps," by Lizette Woodworth Reese and "Little Girl That Mother Used to Be," by Nancy Byrd Turner.

MRS. JOHN KENDRICK BANGS—for "Lincoln's Birthday," and "Lincoln's Birthday, 1918," by John Kendrick Bangs.

BECKLEY CARDY COMPANY—for "Something to be Thankful For" by Clara Denton, from *The Best Thanksgiving Book.*

MORRIS ABEL BEER—for "A Boy of Old Manhattan," and "A Book Is an Enchanted Gate," from *Street Lamps,* published by Harold Vinal at 562 Fifth Avenue.

BOBBS-MERRILL COMPANY—for "A Boy's Mother," from the *Biographical Edition of the Complete Works of James Whitcomb Riley,* copyrighted 1913.

THE CENTURY MAGAZINE AND THE AUTHOR—for "An Offertory," by Mary M. Dodge.

THOMAS CURTIS CLARK—for "The Prophet" and "Lincoln."

CLEVELAND PLAIN DEALER—for "Beneath the Flag."

COLLIER'S—for "Lincoln's Way," by Henry Tyrrel.

JOHN STUART COONLEY—for "Christmas Song" and "Song for Flag Day," by Lydia A. C. Ward.

[v]

Acknowledgments

ROBERT H. DAVIS—for "Roosevelt."

DODD, MEAD & COMPANY—for "Works," by Angela Morgan.

M. A. DONOHUE & COMPANY—for "Theodore Roosevelt," by W. W. Peavyhouse.

GEORGE H. DORAN COMPANY—for "Trees," from *Trees and Other Poems* by Joyce Kilmer, copyrighted 1914, and "Grown Ups," "Mother," and "Fairy Music," from *Fairy Green* by Rose Fyleman, copyrighted 1923.

MAURICE FRANCIS EGAN—for "Shamrock."

C. B. GALBREATH—for "In Flanders Fields"—an Answer.

THEODOSIA GARRISON—for "Saint Jeanne."

MRS. GRACE BOYLAN GELDERT—for "Who Goes There."

GINN & COMPANY—for "Flag of the Free," by Walter Taylor Field.

CHARLES BURTON GOING—for "Columbus."

ARTHUR GUITERMAN—for "Our Colonel."

ELLEN DAY HALE—for "Columbus," by Edward Everett Hale.

HARCOURT, BRACE & COMPANY—for "Flag o' My Land," from *McAroni Ballads*, by T. A. Daly.

HARPER & BROTHERS—for "Our Colonel," by Arthur Guiterman, from *Ballads of Old New York*.

OLIVER HERFORD—for "Thanksgiving Fable."

HENRY HOLT & COMPANY—for "Music," from *Down-Adown-Derry*, by Walter de la Mare, and "Aim Was Song," from *New Hampshire*, by Robert Frost.

HOUGHTON MIFFLIN COMPANY—for "Songs for My Mother," by A. H. Branch; "In Memory of the Soldiers" and "Learning to Play," by A. F. Brown; "Our Dead Heroes," by R. T. Cooke; "If I Were Santa's Little Boy," "Left Out," and "Stars," M. C. Davies; "The Waits," by M. Deland; "We Thank Thee" and "Concord Hymn," R. W. Emerson; "The Flag" and "Day of Joy," by L. Larcom; "The Republic," "Decoration Day," and "Christmas Bells," by H. W. Longfellow; "Washington," by J. R. Lowell; "Coming

of Spring," by Nora Perry; and "Child and the
Year," "Song of Easter," and "Spring," by Celia
Thaxter.

JUDGE—for "Lincoln Leads."

S. E. KISER—for "Memorial Day, 1897."

ALFRED A. KNOPF, INC.—for "Farmer Remembers Lincoln," from *Greenstone Poems* by Witter Bynner.

E. A. HORTON—for "The Flag."

J. B. LIPPINCOTT COMPANY—for "The Flag," by G. H.
Bokar, and "Lincoln's Birthday," by J. K. Bangs.

LITTLE, BROWN & COMPANY—for "At Easter Time" and
"Valentine," by L. E. Richards and "A Book," by
Emily Dickinson.

LOTHROP, LEE & SHEPARD CO.—for "Books Are Keys," by
Emilie Poulsson.

THE MACMILLAN COMPANY—for "Washington's Birthday,"
by M. E. Sangster, from *Little Book of Homespun
Verse.*

EDWIN MARKHAM—for "Lincoln Triumphant," and
"Lincoln, the Man of the People," copyrighted by
Mr. Markham and taken with his permission from his
collected works.

JOHN CLAIR MINOT—for "Little Flags," from *The
Youth's Companion.*

THOMAS BIRD MOSHER and author—for "Taps," by Lizette Woodworth Reese.

W. D. NESBIT—for "Thanksgiving Night."

NEW YORK TIMES—for "Books," by Florence Van Cleve,
"Our Soldier Dead," by A. Kohn, "Unknown Dead,"
by J. R. Rathom, and "Armistice Night," by Curtis
Wheeler.

G. PUTNAM'S SONS—"In Flanders Fields," by J. N. Mc-
Crae.

REILLY & LEE—for "A Creed," from *Poems of Patriotism,*
copyrighted 1918.

E. L. SABIN—for "Easter."

MARGARET E. SANGSTER—for "Washington's Birthday."

C. SCOLLARD—for "For Our Dead."

CHARLES SCRIBNER'S SONS—for "Heart of a Tree," by J.

Acknowledgments

C. Bunner; "Work," by H. Van Dyke; "Jest 'fore Christmas," "Child and Mother," and "Star of the East," by Eugene Field; "Christmas Carol," by J. G. Holland; "Name of Washington," by G. P. Lathrop; "Valiant for Truth," by C. R. Robinson; "The Master," by E. A. Robinson; and "Abraham Lincoln," by R. H. Stoddard.

L. SHERWOOD—for "We Keep Memorial Day," by K. B. Sherwood.

SMALL, MAYNARD & COMPANY—for "Captain, My Captain," by Walt Whitman.

W. P. STAFFORD—for "Lincoln."

F. A. STOKES COMPANY—for "Books, Books," "Books Are Soldiers," "Christopher Columbus," "Columbus," "My Book Holds Many Stories," and "Palos, Spain," reprinted by permission from *For Days and Days: A Year-round Treasury of Verse for Children*, by Annette Wynne, copyright, 1919; "Books," "Easter," "For You, Mother," "Music," and "Spring Song," reprinted by permission from *Shoes of the Wind*, copyright, 1922, and *Poems by a Little Girl*, copyright, 1920, by Hilda Conkling.

THE SURVEY—for "Memorial Day," by W. E. Brooks.

HENRY TYRRELL—for "Lincoln's Way."

MARIE WARMAN—for "Memorial Day," by Cy Warman.

R. WHITAKER—for "Abraham Lincoln."

THE YOUTH'S COMPANION—for "Crown Our Washington," by H. Butterworth, "Flag Goes By," by H. H. Bennett, and "Little Girl That Mother Used to Be," by Nancy Byrd Turner.

YALE UNIVERSITY PRESS—for "To Men Unborn," from *Four Gardens* by D. O. Hamilton.

In some cases it has been extremely difficult to trace the authors and publishers of poems. If by chance we have been guilty of neglect in acknowledging our obligations, we trust that our honest endeavors will be accepted as our apology.

FLORENCE ADAMS
ELIZABETH McCARRICK

Contents

[ix]

Contents

WASHINGTON'S BIRTHDAY

ST. PATRICK'S DAY

ARBOR DAY

BIRD DAY

[x]

Contents

EASTER

MAY DAY

MOTHER'S DAY

MUSIC WEEK

Contents

MEMORIAL DAY

FLAG DAY

INDEPENDENCE DAY

Contents

LABOR DAY

[xiii]

Contents

BOOK WEEK

THANKSGIVING DAY

CHRISTMAS

Contents

Introduction

Teachers and librarians are constantly in search of poems for special occasions and a new collection is always welcome.

"Highdays and Holidays" has been compiled out of the varied and practical experience of two children's librarians.

In common with other compilers, they have not always been able to obtain permission to reprint the poems they wished to include. However, they have made a careful and thorough search, selecting with the younger children especially in mind, and have included a number of holidays which do not appear in other anthologies, such as Roosevelt's Birthday, Armistice Day, Music Week, and Children's Book Week.

I know that this book will be received with genuine delight.

MABEL WILLIAMS
Supervisor of Work with Schools
The New York Public Library

NEW YORK CITY
April, 1927

NEW
YEAR'S
DAY

THE CHILD AND THE YEAR

SAID the child to the youthful year:
    "What hast thou in store for me,
O giver of beautiful gifts! what cheer,
    What joy dost thou bring with thee?"

"My seasons four shall bring
    Their treasures: the winter's snows,
The autumn's store, and the flowers of spring,
    And the summer's perfect rose.

"All these and more shall be thine,
    Dear child—but the last and best
Thyself must earn by a strife divine,
    If thou wouldst be truly blest.

"Wouldst thou know this best gift?
    'Tis a conscience clear and bright,
A peace of mind which the soul can lift
    To an infinite delight.

"Truth, patience, courage, and love,
    If thou unto me canst bring,

I will set thee all earth's ills above,
   O child! and crown thee a king!"

Celia Thaxter

THE DEATH OF THE OLD YEAR

*F*ULL knee-deep lies the winter snow,
   And the winter winds are wearily sighing;
Toll ye the church bell sad and slow,
And tread softly and speak low,
For the old year lies a-dying.
   Old year, you must not die;
   You came to us so readily,
   You lived with us so steadily,
   Old year, you shall not die.

He lieth still; he doth not move;
He will not see the dawn of day,
He hath no other life above.
He gave me a friend, a true, true-love,
And the New Year will take him away.
   Old year, you must not go;
   So long as you have been with us,
   Such joy as you have seen with us,
   Old year, you shall not go.

[4]

The Death of the Old Year

He froth'd with his bumpers to the brim;
A jollier year we shall not see.
But tho' his eyes are waxing dim,
And tho' his foes speak ill of him,
He was a friend to me.
    Old year, you shall not die;
        We did so laugh and cry with you,
        I've half a mind to die with you,
        Old year, if you must die.

He was so full of joke and jest,
But all his merry quips are o'er.
To see him die, across the waste
His son and heir doth ride post-haste,
But he'll be dead before.
    Every one for his own;
        The night is starry and cold, my friend,
        And the New Year blithe and bold, my friend,
        Comes up to take his own.

How hard he breathes!   Over the snow
I heard just now the crowing cock,
The shadows flicker to and fro;
The cricket chirps! the light burns low!
'Tis nearly twelve o'clock.

New Year

Shake hands, before you die;
Old year, we'll dearly rue for you:
What is it we can do for you?
Speak out before you die.

His face is growing sharp and thin
Alack! our friend is gone!
Close up his eyes; tie up his chin;
Step from the corpse, and let him in
That standeth there alone.
    And waiteth at the door.
    There's a new foot on the floor, my friend,
    And a new face at the door, my friend,
    A new face at the door.

Alfred, Lord Tennyson

NEW YEAR

W HO comes dancing over the snow,
    His soft little feet all bare and rosy?
Open the door, though the wild winds blow,
    Take the child in and make him cosy.
Take him in and hold him dear,
He is the wonderful glad New Year.

Dinah Maria Mulock

NEW YEAR

*O*VER the threshold a gallant new-comer
    Steppeth with tread that is royal to see;
White as the winter-time, rosy as summer,
    Hope in his eyes, and with laugh ringing free.
Lo! in his hands there are gifts overflowing,
    Promises, prophecies, come in his train;
O'er him the dawn in its beauty is glowing,
    Banishing shadows of sorrow and pain.

Oh, welcome, New Year! with your stainless
    white pages,
    Though we may blot them ere long with our
      tears;
So it has been through the long passing ages,
    Worn with the footprints of close crowding
      years.
Welcome, sweet Year! may the full-handed
    hours
    Find us like servants, trusty and true,
Using with earnest devotion our powers
    To be worthy our Master and worthy of you.

Unknown

[7]

NEW YEAR SONG

*T*HEY say that the Year is old and gray,
    That his eyes are dim with sorrow;
But what care we, though he pass away?
    For the New Year comes to-morrow.

No sighs have we for the roses fled,
    No tears for the vanished summer;
Fresh flowers will spring where the old are dead,
    To welcome the glad newcomer.

He brings us a gift from the beautiful land
    We see, in our rosy dreaming,
Where the wonderful castles of fancy stand
    In magical sunshine gleaming.

Then sing, young hearts that are full of cheer,
    With never a thought of sorrow;
The old goes out, but the glad young year
    Comes merrily in to-morrow.

Mrs. Emily Huntington Miller

ON THE THRESHOLD

RING out, O bells!   Ring silver sweet o'er
hill and moor and fell!
In mellow echoes let your chimes their hopeful
story tell.
Ring out, ring out, all-jubilant, the joyous, glad
refrain;
"A bright new year, a glad new year, hath come
to us again!"

Ah! who can say how much of joy within it there
may be
Stored up for us who listen now to your sweet
melody!
Good-bye, Old Year!   Tried, trusty friend, thy
tale at last is told;
O New Year! write thou thine for us in lines of
brightest gold.

The flowers of spring must bloom at last, when
gone the winter's snow;
God grant that after sorrow past, we all some
joy may know.
Though tempest-tossed our bark awhile on Life's
rough waves may be,

There comes a day of calm at last, when we the
haven see.

Then ring, ring on, O pealing bells! there's
music in the sound.
Ring on, ring on, and still ring on, and wake
the echoes round,
The while we wish, both for ourselves and all
whom we hold dear,
That God may gracious be to us in this the bright
New Year!

A. H. Baldwin

RING OUT, WILD BELLS

RING out, wild bells, to the wild sky,
The flying cloud, the frosty light;
The year is dying in the night;
Ring out, wild bells, and let him die.

Ring out the old, ring in the new,
Ring, happy bells, across the snow;
The year is going, let him go;
Ring out the false, ring in the true.

Ring out the grief that saps the mind,
For those that here we see no more;

Ring Out, Wild Bells

Ring out the feud of rich and poor,
Ring in redress to all mankind.

Ring out a slowly dying cause,
    And ancient forms of party strife;
    Ring in the nobler modes of life,
With sweeter manners, purer laws.

Ring out the want, the care, the sin,
    The faithless coldness of the times;
    Ring out, ring out my mournful rhymes,
But ring the fuller minstrel in.

Ring out false pride in place and blood,
    The civic slander and the spite;
    Ring in the love of truth and right,
Ring in the common love of good.

Ring out old shapes of foul disease;
    Ring out the narrowing lust of gold;
    Ring out the thousand wars of old,
Ring in the thousand years of peace.

Ring in the valiant man and free,
    The larger heart, the kindlier hand;
    Ring out the darkness of the land,
Ring in the Christ that is to be.

Alfred, Lord Tennyson

LINCOLN'S BIRTHDAY

ABRAHAM LINCOLN

*T*HIS man whose homely face you look upon,
  Was one of nature's masterful, great men;
Born with strong arms, that unfought battles
    won;
  Direct of speech, and cunning with the pen.
Chosen for large designs, he had the art
  Of winning with his humor, and he went
Straight to his mark, which was the human heart;
  Wise, too, for what he could not break he
    bent.
Upon his back a more than Atlas-load,
  The burden of the Commonwealth, was laid;
He stooped, and rose up to it, though the road
  Shot suddenly downwards, not a whit dis-
    mayed.
Hold, warriors, councillors, kings! All now give
    place
To this dear benefactor of the race.

Richard Henry Stoddard

ABRAHAM LINCOLN

*T*HERE is no name in all our country's story
  So loved as his today:
No name that so unites the things of glory
  With life's plain, common way.

Poor as the poorest were his days' beginnings,
  The earth-floored cabin home.
And yet, compared with his, our rich man's win-
    nings
Are fleeting as the foam.

His was a tragedy such deeps concealing
  All eyes with his grow dim.
And his a humor so sincerely healing
  The whole world laughs with him.

He knew the doubter's doubt, the restless heav-
    ing
  Of the swift waves of youth.
He knew the calm of faith, the strong believing
  Of him who lives the truth.

So manifold his life, the great-souled Lincoln
  Makes every life his own.
Therefore of all our heroes whom we think on
  He has a place alone.

Robert Whitaker

[16]

DEATH OF LINCOLN

OH, slow to smite and swift to spare,
    Gentle and merciful and just!
Who, in the fear of God, didst bear
    The sword of power, a nation's trust!

In sorrow by thy bier we stand,
    Amid the awe that hushes all,
And speak the anguish of a land
    That shook with horror at thy fall.

Thy task is done; the bonds are free;
    We bear thee to an honored grave;
Whose proudest monument shall be
    The broken fetters of the slave.

Pure was thy life; its bloody close
    Hath placed thee with the sons of light,
Among the noble host of those
    Who perished in the cause of Right.

William Cullen Bryant

[17]

GREAT OAK

SOME men are born, while others seem to
grow
From out the soil, like towering trees that spread
Their strong, broad limbs in shelter overhead
When tempest storms, protecting all below.

Lincoln, Great Oak of a Nation's life,
Rose from the soil, with all its virgin power
Emplanted in him for the fateful hour,
When he might save a Nation in its strife.

Bennett Chapple

LINCOLN

WISE with the wisdom of ages
Shrewd as a man of trade,
Grim as the prophets and sages,
Keen as a damask blade;

Firm as a granite ribbed mountain,
Tender as woman's song,
Gay as a scintillant fountain—
Yet was he oaken-strong.

[20]

Here, the wonder of æons!
Born unto pain and strife;
Dead, 'mid a thousand pæans,
Deathless, he enters life.

Thomas Curtis Clark

LINCOLN

$\mathcal{S}$AY— if men asked for him—he has gone
home,
Home to the hearts of all that love their kind;
And they that seek him there, henceforth shall
find
Their man of men—in all men's hearts at home.
The Mother made him from her common loam,
And from her world-wide harvest filled his mind,
Poured by all paths, that from all quarters
wind,
As in the old days all highways poured to Rome.
She said: "I make a universal man,
Warmed with all laughter, tempered with all
tears,
Whose word and deed shall have the force of
fate.
I made not seven in all, since time began,

Of men like these.   They last a thousand years,
They have the power to will, the will to wait."

Wendell Phillips Stafford

LINCOLN LEADS

*A*CROSS the page of history,
　　As in a looking glass
Or on a moving-picture screen,
　　The Nation's heroes pass;
With sword and mace and pen they pace
　　In epaulets and braid,
And some, with ruffles at their wrists,
　　In linen fine arrayed.

But at the long procession's head,
　　In loose ill-fitting clothes,
A lanky woodsman with an axe
　　Upon his shoulder goes;
In every patriotic heart
　　The figure lean and tall
Is shrined beside the starry flag
　　For Lincoln leads them all.

Minna Irving

LINCOLN'S WAY

L INCOLN arose! the masterful great man,
 Girt with rude grandeur, quelling doubt
and fear—
A more than King, yet in whose veins there ran
 The red blood of the people, warm, sincere,
 Blending of Puritan and Cavalier.

Henry Tyrrell

LINCOLN, THE MAN OF THE PEOPLE

W HEN the Norn Mother saw the Whirlwind
 Hour
Greatening and darkening as it hurried on,
She left the Heaven of Heroes and came down
To make a man to meet the mortal need.
She took the tried clay of the common road—
Clay warm yet with the genial heat of Earth,
Dasht through it all a strain of prophecy,
Tempered the heap with thrill of human tears
Then mixt a laughter with the serious stuff.
Into the shape she breathed a flame to light
That tender, tragic, ever-changing face;
And laid on him a sense of the Mystic Powers,
Moving—all husht—behind the mortal vail.

Here was a man to hold against the world,
A man to match the mountains and the sea.

The color of the ground was in him, the red earth,
The smack and tang of elemental things:
The rectitude and patience of the cliff,
The good-will of the rain that loves all leaves,
The friendly welcome of the wayside well,
The courage of the bird that dares the sea,
The gladness of the wind that shakes the corn.
The pity of the snow that hides all scars,
The secrecy of streams that make their way
Under the mountain to the rifted rock,
The tolerance and equity of light
That gives as freely to the shrinking flower
As to the great oak flaring to the wind—
To the grave's low hill as to the Matterhorn
That shoulders out the sky. Sprung from the
     West,
He drank the valorous youth of a new world.
The strength of virgin forests braced his mind,
The hush of spacious prairies stilled his soul.
His words were oaks in acorns; and his thoughts
Were roots that firmly gript the granite truth.

Up from log cabin to the Capitol,

One fire was on his spirit, one resolve—
To send the keen ax to the root of wrong,
Clearing a free way for the feet of God,
The eyes of conscience testing every stroke,
To make his deed the measure of a man.
He built the rail-pile as he built the State,
Pouring his splendid strength through every
    blow:
The grip that swung the ax in Illinois
Was on the pen that set a people free.

So came the Captain with the mighty heart;
And when the judgment thunders split the
    house,
Wrenching the rafters from their ancient rest,
He held the ridgepole up, and spikt again
The rafters of the Home. He held his place—
Held the long purpose like a growing tree—
Held on through blame and faltered not at
    praise—
Held on in calm rough-hewn sublimity.
And when he fell in whirlwind, he went down
As when a lordly cedar, green with boughs,
Goes down with a great shout upon the hills,
And leaves a lonesome place against the sky.

Edwin Markham

LINCOLN TRIUMPHANT

*L*INCOLN is not dead. He lives
　　In all that pities and forgives.
He has arisen and sheds a fire
That makes America aspire.

Even now as, when in life, he led,
He leads us onward from the dead;
Yes, over the whole wide world he bends
To make the world a world of friends.

Edwin Markham

LINCOLN'S BIRTHDAY

A SACRED day is this—
　　A day to bless;
A day that leads to bliss
　　Through bitterness.
For on this day of days,
　　One wondrous morn,
In far off forest ways,
　　Was Lincoln born!

Lincoln's Birthday

Who supped the cup of tears,
    Who ate the bread
Of sorrow and of fears,
    Of war and dread;
Yet from this feast of woes,
    His people's pride,
A loved immortal rose
    All glorified!

John Kendrick Bangs

LINCOLN'S BIRTHDAY—1918

WHEN over-burdened with its care
    My soul seems yielding to despair,
I think of him to whom today
All men a golden tribute pay.

Who in the midst of trials sore
His burden uncomplaining bore,
And out of bitterness ran on
To splendid laurels nobly won;

And from the thought of him I too
Gain confidence and courage true,
And faith sublime, that thro' the night
Mine eyes will find their way to light.

John Kendrick Bangs

MAN OF PEACE

*W*HAT winter holiday is this?
   In Time's great calendar,
Marked in the rubric of the saints,
   And with a soldier's star,
Here stands the name of one who lived
   To serve the common weal,
With humor tender as a prayer
   And honor firm as steel.

Born in the fulness of the days
   Up from the teeming soil,
By the world-molten reared and schooled
   In reverence and toil,
He stands the test of all life's best
   Through play, defeat, or strain;
Never a moment was he found
   Unlovable nor vain.

O South, bring all your chivalry;
   And West, give all your heart;
And East, your old untarnished dreams
   Of progress and of art!

Bid waste and war to be no more,
  Bid wanton riot cease;
At your command give Lincoln's land
  To Paradise,—to peace.

Bliss Carman

THE MASTER

A FLYING word from here and there
    Had sown the name at which we
sneered,
But soon the name was everywhere,
  To be reviled and then revered:
A presence to be loved and feared,
  We cannot hide it, or deny
That we, the gentlemen who jeered,
  May be forgotten by and by.

He came when days were perilous
  And hearts of men were sore beguiled;
And having made his note of us,
  He pondered and was reconciled.
Was ever master yet so mild
  As he, and so untamable?
We doubted, even when he smiled,
  Not knowing what he knew so well.

[29]

The Master

He knew that undeceiving fate
    Would shame us whom he served unsought;
He knew that he must wince and wait—
    The jest of those for whom he fought;
He knew devoutly what he thought
    Of us and of our ridicule:
He knew that we must all be taught
    Like little children in a school.

We gave a glamour to the task
    That he encountered and saw through,
But little of us did he ask,
    And little did we ever do.
And what appears if we review
    The season when we railed and chaffed?
It is the face of one who knew
    That we were learning while we laughed.

The face that in our vision feels
    Again the venom that we flung,
Transfigured to the world reveals
    The vigilance to which we clung.
Shrewd, hallowed, harassed, and among
    The mysteries that are untold,
The face we see was never young,
    Nor could it ever have been old.

The Master

For he, to whom we have applied
  Our shopman's test of age and worth,
Was elemental when he died,
  As he was ancient at his birth:
The saddest among kings of earth,
  Bowed with a galling crown, this man
Met rancor with a cryptic mirth,
  Laconic—and Olympian.

The love, the grandeur, and the fame
  Are bounded by the world alone;
The calm, the smouldering, and the flame
  Of awful patience were his own:
With him they are forever flown
  Past all our fond self-shadowings,
Wherewith we cumber the Unknown
  As with inept Icarian wings.

For we were not as other men:
  'Twas ours to soar and his to see.
But we are coming down again,
  And we shall come down pleasantly;
Nor shall we longer disagree
  On what it is to be sublime,
But flourish in our perigee
  And have one Titan at a time.

Edwin Arlington Robinson

[31]

O CAPTAIN! MY CAPTAIN!

O CAPTAIN! my Captain! our fearful trip
    is done.
The ship has weather'd every rack, the prize we
    sought is won,
The port is near, the bells I hear, the people all
    exulting,
While follow eyes the steady keel, the vessel
    grim and daring;
  But O heart! heart! heart!
   O the bleeding drops of red,
  Where on the deck my Captain lies,
   Fallen cold and dead.

O Captain! my Captain! rise up and hear the
    bells;
Rise up—for you the flag is flung—for you the
    bugle trills,
For you bouquets and ribbon'd wreaths—for
    you the shores a-crowding,
For you they call, the swaying mass, their eager
    faces turning;

On Lincoln's Birthday

Here, Captain! dear father!
    This arm beneath your head!
It is some dream that on the deck,
    You've fallen cold and dead.

My Captain does not answer, his lips are pale
    and still,
My father does not feel my arm, he has no pulse
    nor will,
The ship is anchor'd safe and sound, its voyage
    closed and done,
From fearful trip the victor ship comes in with
    object won;
    Exult, O shores! and ring, O bells;
    But I with mournful tread,
Walk the deck my Captain lies,
    Fallen cold and dead.

Walt Whitman

ON LINCOLN'S BIRTHDAY

A DAY of joy, a holiday!
    A day in festal colors drest
To honor one who knew not play,
    Nor ever tasted rest!

[33]

On Lincoln's Birthday

A man of sorrows and of tears,
  Would we might bring to you
Back through the pathway of dead years
  One touch of comfort true.

Would that your eyes might penetrate
  The shadows in between
Through all the clouds of war and hate
  And mists that intervene.

Into the hearts of all the throng
  Of living men, to find
Your name and fame the first among
  The treasures of mankind!

John Kendrick Bangs

VALENTINE'S
DAY

O MISTRESS MINE

O MISTRESS MINE, where are you
  roaming?
O, stay and hear! your true-love's coming
  That can sing both high and low;
Trip no further, pretty sweeting,
Journeys end in lovers' meeting,—
  Every wise man's son doth know.

What is love? 'Tis not hereafter;
Present mirth hath present laughter;
  What's to come is still unsure:
In delay there lies no plenty,—
Then—come kiss me, Sweet-and-Twenty,
  Youth's a stuff will not endure.

William Shakespeare

A VALENTINE

O LITTLE loveliest lady mine,
  What shall I send for your valentine?
Summer and flowers are far away;
Gloomy old Winter is king to-day;

[37]

Rosy Apple, Lemon, or Pear

Buds will not blow, and sun will not shine:
What shall I do for a valentine?

I've searched the gardens all through and
    through
For a bud to tell of my love so true;
But buds are asleep and blossoms are dead,
And the snow beats down on my poor little
    head:
So, little loveliest lady mine,
Here is my heart for your valentine!

Laura E. Richards

ROSY APPLE, LEMON, OR PEAR

*R*OSY apple, lemon, or pear,
   Rosy apple, lemon, or pear,
Bunch of roses she shall wear:
Gold and silver by her side,
I know who will be the bride.
Take her by her lily-white hand,
Lead her to the altar;
Give her kisses,—one, two, three,—
Mother's runaway daughter.

Unknown

LAVENDER'S BLUE

*L*AVENDER'S blue, dilly dilly, lavender's
    green,
When I am king, dilly dilly, you shall be queen.
Who told you so, dilly dilly, who told you so?
'Twas mine own heart, dilly dilly, that told me
    so.
Call up your men, dilly dilly, set them to work,
Some with a rake, dilly dilly, some with a fork,
Some to make hay, dilly dilly, some to thresh
    corn,
Whilst you and I, dilly dilly, keep ourselves
    warm.

Unknown

SONG

*G*OOD MORROW, 'tis St. Valentine's day,
    All in the morning betime,
And I a maid at your window,
    To be your Valentine.

William Shakespeare

[39]

Washington's Birthday

CROWN OUR WASHINGTON

*A*RISE—'Tis the day of our Washington's
    glory,
  The garlands uplift for our liberties won;
Forever let Youth tell the patriot's story,
    Whose sword swept for freedom the fields of
    the sun!
        Not with gold, nor with gems
        But with evergreens vernal,
And the banners of stars that the continent span,
    Crown, crown we the chief of the heroes
    eternal,
Who lifted his sword for the birthright of man!

He gave us a nation; to make it immortal
    He laid down for freedom the sword that he
    drew,
And faith leads us on through the uplifting
    portal
    Of the glories of peace and our destinies new.
        Not with gold, nor with gems,
        But with evergreens vernal,
And the flag that the nations of liberty span,

Crown, crown him the chief of the heroes
　　eternal,
Who laid down his sword for the birthright of
　　man!

Lead, Face of the Future, serene in thy beauty,
　　Till o'er the dead heroes the peace star shall
　　　　gleam,
Till Right shall be might in the counsels of duty,
　　And the service of man be life's glory
　　　　supreme.
　　　　　　Not with gold, nor with gems,
　　　　　　But with evergreens vernal,
And the flags that the nations in brotherhood
　　span,
　　Crown, crown we the chief of the heroes
　　　　eternal,
Whose honor was gained by his service to man!

Hezekiah Butterworth

GEORGE WASHINGTON

*T*HIS was the man God gave us when the hour
　　Proclaimed the dawn of Liberty begun;
Who dared a deed and died when it was done
Patient in triumph, temperate in power,—

George Washington

Not striving like the Corsican to tower
To heaven, nor like Philip's greater son
To win the world and weep for worlds unwon,
Or leave the star to revel in the flower.

The lives that serve the eternal verities
Alone do mould mankind.   Pleasure and pride
Sparkle awhile and perish, as the spray
Smoking across the crests of cavernous seas
Is impotent to hasten or delay
The everlasting surges of the tide.

John Hall

GEORGE WASHINGTON

(A recitation for five small boys. Let each boy hold in
his right hand a card with date, lifting it high during his
recitation.)

1732 In Seventeen Hundred Thirty-Two
  George Washington was born;
   Truth, goodness, skill, and glory high,
  His whole life did adorn.

1775 In Seventeen Hundred Seventy-Five,
  The chief command he took
  Of all the army in the State
  And ne'er his flag forsook.

1783 In Seventeen Hundred Eighty-Three
  Retired to private life
 He saw his much-loved country free
  From battle and from strife.

1789 In Seventeen Hundred Eighty-Nine
  The country with one voice,
 Proclaimed him President to shine,
  Blessed by the people's choice.

1799 In Seventeen Hundred Ninety-Nine
  The nation's tears were shed,
 To see the Patriot life resign,
  And sleep among the dead.

All As "first in war, and first in peace,"
  As patriot, father, friend,
 He will be blessed till time shall cease,
  And earthly life shall end.

Unknown

LIKE WASHINGTON

*W*E cannot all be Washingtons,
  And have our birthdays celebrated;
But we can love the things he loved,
 And we can hate the things he hated.

[46]

He loved the truth, he hated lies,
　He minded what his mother taught him,
And every day he tried to do
　The simple duties that it brought him.

Perhaps the reason little folks
　Are sometimes great when they grow taller,
Is just because, like Washington,
　They do their best when they are smaller.

Unknown

THE NAME OF WASHINGTON

S͡ONS of the youth and the truth of a nation,
　Ye that are met to remember the man
Whose valor gave birth to a people's salvation,
　Honor him now; set his name in the van,
　　A nobleness to try for,
　　A name to live and die for—
　　　The name of Washington.

Calmly his face shall look down through the
　　ages—
　Sweet yet severe with a spirit of warning;
Charged with the wisdom of saints and of sages;

[47]

The Name of Washington

Quick with the light of a life-giving morning.
   A majesty to try for,
   A name to live and die for—
      The name of Washington!

Though faction may rack us, or party divide us,
   And bitterness break the gold links of our
      story,
Our father and leader is ever beside us.
   Live and forgive! But forget not the glory
      Of him whose height we try for,
      A name to live and die for—
         The name of Washington!

Still in his eyes shall be mirrored our fleeting
   Days, with the image of days long ended;
Still shall those eyes give, immortally, greeting
   Unto the souls from his spirit descended.
      His grandeur we will try for,
      His name we'll live and die for—
         The name of Washington!

George Parsons Lathrop

OUR WASHINGTON

O SON of Virginia, thy mem'ry divine
Forever will halo this country of thine,
Not hero alone in the battle's wild strife,
But hero in ev'ry detail of thy life.
So noble, unselfish, heroic, and true,
A God given gift to thy country were you;
And lovingly, tenderly guarding thy shrine,
Columbia points proudly, and says: "He is
mine."

Thy courage upheld us, the judgment sustained,
Thy spirit stood proof when discouragement
reigned,
Thy justice unerring all bias withstood,
Thy thought never self, but thy loved country's
good.
And thy country will never, till time is no more.
Cease to cherish the sleeper on yon river's shore;
And every fair daughter and ev'ry brave son
She will tell of the greatness of her Washington.

O hero immortal! O spirit divine!
What glory eternal, what homage is thine!
Forever increasing will be thy renown,

With the stars of Columbia that gleam in thy
    crown.
The God who guards liberty gave thee to earth,
Forever we'll honor thy heaven-sent birth.
E'en heaven itself has one gladness the more,
That our hands shall clasp thine on eternity's
    shore.

Then sleep, sweetly sleep, by the river's calm
    run;
Thy fame will live on in the land thou hast won;
To Potomac's soft music then slumber serene,
The spirit of freedom will keep the spot green;
And so long as time echoes the hour of thy birth,
We will pay loving tribute and praise to thy
    worth,
And pledge to keep spotless the freedom you
    gave,
And the land that is hallowed by Washington's
    grave.

Eliza W. Durbin

THE TWENTY–SECOND OF FEBRUARY

*P*ALE is the February sky,
　　And brief the mid-day's sunny hours;
The wind-swept forest seems to sigh
　　For the sweet time of leaves and flowers.

Yet has no month a prouder day,
　　Not even when the summer broods
O'er meadows in their fresh array,
　　Or autumn tints the glowing woods.

For this chill season now again
　　Brings, in its annual round, the morn
When, greatest of the sons of men,
　　Our glorious Washington was born.

Lo, where, beneath an icy shield,
　　Calmly the mighty Hudson flows!
By snow-clad fell and frozen field,
　　Broadening the lordly river goes.

The wildest storm that sweeps through space,
　　And rends the oak with sudden force,
Can raise no ripple on his face,
　　Or slacken his majestic course.

Thus, 'mid the wreck of thrones, shall live
　　Unmarred, undimmed, our hero's fame,
And years succeeding years shall give
　　Increase of honors to his name.

William Cullen Bryant

WASHINGTON

*W*ASHINGTON, the brave, the wise, the
　　the good,
Supreme in war, in council, and in peace,
Valiant without ambition, discreet without fear,
　　Confident without presumption.

In disaster, calm; in success, moderate: in all,
　　himself.
The hero, the patriot, the Christian.
The father of nations, the friend of mankind,
Who, when he had won all, renounced all,
Then sought in the bosom of his family and of
　　nature, retirement,
And in the hope of religion, immortality.

Inscription at Mt. Vernon

[52]

WASHINGTON

$\mathcal{S}$OLDIER and statesman, rarest unison;
   High-poised example of great duties done
Simply as breathing, a world's honors worn
As life's indifferent gifts to all men born;
Dumb for himself, unless it were to God,
But for his barefoot soldiers eloquent,
Tramping the snow to corral where they trod,
Held by his awe in hollow-eyed content;
Modest, yet firm as Nature's self; unblamed
Save by the men his nobler temper shamed;
Never seduced through show of present good
By other than unsettling lights to steer
New-trimmed in Heaven, nor than his steadfast
   mood
More steadfast, far from rashness as from fear;
Rigid, but with himself first, grasping still
In swerveless poise the wave-beat helm of will;
Not honored then or now because he wooed
The popular voice, but that he still withstood;
Broad-minded, higher souled, there is but one
Who was all this and ours, and all men's—
   Washington.

James Russell Lowell

WASHINGTON

*W*E all will honor Washington,
    The first in war when wrong was done.
The first in peace when Freedom came
To crown him with immortal fame,
The first in all our hearts today,
To bind us all as one for aye,
While battle and freedom lead us on
We all will honor Washington.

Unknown

WASHINGTON

O NOBLE brow, so wise in thought,
    O heart, so true!   O soul unbought,
O eye, so keen to pierce the night
And guide the "ship of state" aright!

O life, so simple, grand and free,
The humblest still may turn to thee,
O king, uncrowned!   O prince of men!
When shall we see thy like again?

Washington's Birthday

The century, just passed away,
Has felt the impress of thy sway.
While youthful hearts have stronger grown
And made thy patriot zeal their own.
In marble hall or lowly cot
Thy name has never been forgot.
The world itself is richer far,
For the clear shining of a star.
And loyal hearts in years to run
Shall turn to thee, O Washington.

Mary Wingate

WASHINGTON'S BIRTHDAY

*A*LL hail, thou glorious morn
 When Washington was born!
 All hail to thee!
Whether thy skies be bright,
Or veiled in clouds of night,
To thee in joyous right
 Our song shall be.

All come with glad acclaim,
To sing and praise thy name,
 O Washington!

[55]

Washington's Birthday

O'er all this land so free,
Hearts turn with pride to thee,
Champion of liberty,
    Columbia's son.

Charles S. Davis

WASHINGTON'S BIRTHDAY

'*T*IS splendid to live so grandly
    That long after you are gone,
The things you did are remembered,
    And recounted under the sun;
To live so bravely and purely,
    That a nation stops on its way
And once a year with banner and drum,
    Keeps its thought of your natal day.

'Tis splendid to have a record,
    So white and free from stain
That, held to the light, it shows no blot
    Though tested and tried again;
That age to age forever
    Repeats its story of love,
And your birthday lives in a nation's heart
    All other days above.

Washington's Birthday

And this is Washington's glory,
    A steadfast soul and true
Who stood for his country's honor
    When his country's days were few.
And now when its days are many,
    And its flag of stars is flung
To the breeze in defiant challenge,
    His name is on every tongue.

Yes; it's splendid to live so bravely,
    To be so great and strong
That your memory is like a tocsin
    To rally the foes of the wrong.
To live so proudly and purely
    That your people pause in their way,
And year by year, with banner and drum,
    Keep the thought of your natal day.

Margaret E. Sangster

ST. PATRICK'S DAY

ST. PATRICK

*W*ANDERED from the Antrim hills,
    Wandered from Killalas rills,
Patrick heard upon the breeze
Voices from the Irish seas.
Folk of Fochlad called to him
From their forest deep and dim:
And in vision little hands
Beckoned from the Irish lands,
Where the western billows spoke
With the Druid groves of oak.

Unknown

THE SHAMROCK

*T*HERE'S a dear little plant that grows in our
    isle,
  'Twas St. Patrick himself, sure, that set it;
And the sun on his labour with pleasure did
    smile,
  And with dew from his eye often wet it.
It thrives through the bog,
        through the brake,
        through the nureland

[61]

The Shamrock

And he called it the dear little shamrock of
    Ireland.
The sweet little shamrock, the dear little
    shamrock,
The sweet little, green little shamrock of Ireland.

This dear little plant that springs from our soil,
    When its three little leaves are extended,
Denotes from one stalk we together should toil,
    And ourselves by ourselves be befriended.
And still through the bog,
        through the brake,
        through the nureland,
From one root should branch, like the shamrock
    of Ireland.
The sweet little shamrock, the dear little sham-
    rock,
The sweet little, green little shamrock of
    Ireland.

Andrew Cherry

THE SHAMROCK

*W*HEN April rains make flowers bloom
    And Johnny-jump-ups come to light,
And clouds of color and perfume
    Float from the orchards pink and white,
I see my shamrock in the rain,
    An emerald spray with raindrops set,
Like jewels on Spring's coronet,
    So fair, and yet it breathes of pain.

The shamrock on an older shore
    Sprang from a rich and sacred soil
Where saint and hero lived of yore,
    And where their sons in sorrow toil;
And here, transplanted, it to me
    Seems weeping for the soil it left:
The diamonds that all others see
    Are tears drawn from its heart bereft.

When April rain makes flowers grow
    And sparkles on their tiny buds
That in June nights will over-blow
    And fill the world with scented floods,

The Shamrock

The lonely shamrock in our land—
  So fine among the clover leaves—
For the old springtimes often grieves,—
  I feel its tears upon my hand.

Maurice Francis Eagen

THE SHAMROCK

*L*ONG may the shamrock,
  The plant that blooms for ever,
With the rose combined,
And the thistle twined,
Defy the strength of foes to sever.
Firm be the triple league they form,
Despite all change of weather
In sunshine, darkness, calm or storm,
Still may they fondly grow together.

Unknown

THE WEARIN' O' THE GREEN

O PADDY DEAR! an' did ye hear the news
  that's goin' round?
The shamrock is by law forbid to grow on Irish
  ground!

The Wearin' o' the Green

No more St. Patrick's day we'll keep, his color
    can't be seen,
For there's a cruel law agin the wearin' o' the
    green!
I met wid Napper Tandy, and he took me by the
    hand,
And he said, "How's poor Ould Ireland, and
    how does she stand?"
She's the most disthressful country that iver yet
    was seen,
For they're hangin' men and women there for
    wearin' o' the green.

An' if the color we must wear is England's cruel
    red,
Let it remind us of the blood that Ireland has
    shed;
Then pull the shamrock from your hat, and
    throw it on the sod,—
And never fear, 'twill take root there, tho' under
    foot 'tis trod!
When law can stop the blades of grass from
    growin' as they grow,
And when the leaves in summer-time their color
    dare not show,

The Wearin' o' the Green

Then will I change the color, too, I wear in my
    caubeen,
But till that day, plaze God, I'll stick to wearin'
    o' the green.

Unknown

ARBOR
DAY

ARBOR DAY SONG

OF nature broad and free,
    Of grass and flower and tree,
  Sing we today.
God hath pronounced it good,
So we, his creatures would
Offer to field and wood
  Our heartfelt lay.

To all that meets the eye,
In earth, or in sky,
  Tribute we bring.
Barren this world would be,
Bereft of shrub and tree;
Now Gracious Lord to Thee,
  Praises we sing.

May we Thy hand behold,
As bud and leaf unfold,
  See but Thy thought;
Nor heedlessly destroy,
Nor pass unnoticed by;

But be our constant joy
   All Thou hast wrought.

As each small bud and flower
Speaks of the Maker's power,
   Tells of His love;
So we, Thy children dear,
Would live from year to year,
Show forth Thy goodness here,
   And then above.

Mary A. Heermans

AN ARBOR DAY TREE

*D*EAR little tree that we plant to-day,
   What will you be when we're old and gray?
"The savings bank of the squirrel and mouse,
   For robin and wren an apartment house,
The dressing-room of the butterfly's ball,
The locust's and katydid's concert hall,
   The schoolboy's ladder in pleasant June,
   The schoolgirl's tent in the July noon,
And my leaves shall whisper them merrily
A tale of the children who planted me."

Unknown

[70]

THE HEART OF THE TREE

*W*HAT does he plant who plants a tree?
     He plants the friend of sun and sky;
He plants the flag of breezes free;
The shaft of beauty, towering high;
He plants a home to heaven anigh
   For song and mother-croon of bird
   In hushed and happy twilight heard—
The treble of heaven's harmony—
These things he plants who plants a tree.

What does he plant who plants a tree?
   He plants cool shade and tender rain,
And seed and bud of days to be,
And years that fade and flush again;
He plants the glory of the plain;
   He plants the forest's heritage;
   The harvest of a coming age;
The joy that unborn eyes shall see—
These things he plants who plants a tree.

What does he plant who plants a tree?
   He plants, in sap and leaf and wood,
In love of home and loyalty
And far-cast thought of civic good—

[71]

The Oak

His blessings on the neighborhood
　　Who in the hollow of His hand
　　Holds all the growth of all our land—
A nation's growth from sea to sea
Stirs in his heart who plants a tree.

Henry Cuyler Bunner

THE OAK

A GLORIOUS tree is the old gray oak:
　　He has stood for a thousand years;
　　Has stood and frowned
　　On the trees around,
　Like a king among his peers;
As round their king they stand, so now,
　When the flowers their pale leaves fold,
The tall trees round him stand, arrayed
　In their robes of purple and gold.

He has stood like a tower
Through sun and shower,
And dared the winds to battle;
　He has heard the hail,
　As from plates of mail,
From his own limbs shaken, rattle;

[72]

He has tossed them about, and shorn the tops
　(When the storm has roused his might)
Of the forest-trees, as a strong man doth
　The heads of his foes in fight.

George Hill

THE TREE

*T*HE Tree's early leaf-buds were bursting
　　their brown;
"Shall I take them away?" said the Frost
　sweeping down.
　　　"No, leave them alone
　　　Till the blossoms have grown,"
Prayed the Tree, while he trembled from root-
　let to crown.

The Tree bore his blossoms, and all the birds
　sung:
"Shall I take them away?" said the Wind, as
　he swung.
　　　"No, leave them alone
　　　Till the berries have grown,"
Said the Tree, while his leaflets quivering hung.

Trees

The Tree bore his fruit in the mid-summer glow:
Said the girl, "May I gather thy berries now?"
    "Yes, all thou canst see:
    Take them; all are for thee,"
Said the Tree, while he bent down his laden
  boughs low.

Bjornstern Bjornson

TREES

I THINK that I shall never see
  A poem lovely as a tree.

A tree whose hungry mouth is prest
Against the earth's sweet flowing breast.

A tree that looks at God all day
And lifts her leafy arms to pray;

A tree that may in summer wear
A nest of robins in her hair;

Upon whose bosom snow has lain,
Who intimately lives with rain.

Poems are made by fools like me,
But only God can make a tree.

Joyce Kilmer

WHAT DO WE PLANT WHEN WE PLANT THE TREE?

WHAT do we plant when we plant the tree?
　　We plant the ship which will cross the
　sea,
We plant the mast to carry the sails,
We plant the planks to withstand the gales—
The keel, the keelson, and beam and knee,—
We plant the ship when we plant the tree.

What do we plant when we plant the tree?
We plant the houses for you and me.
We plant the rafters, the shingles, the floors,
We plant the studding, the lath, the doors,
The beams and siding, all parts that be,
We plant the house when we plant the tree.

What do we plant when we plant the tree?
A thousand things that we daily see.
We plant the spire that out-towers the crag,
We plant the staff for our country's flag,
We plant the shade from the hot sun free;
We plant all these when we plant the tree.

Henry Abbey

WOODMAN, SPARE THAT TREE!

*W*OODMAN, spare that tree!
Touch not a single bough!
In youth it sheltered me,
And I'll protect it now.
'Twas my forefather's hand
That placed it near his cot;
There, woodman, let it stand,
Thy ax shall harm it not.

That old familiar tree,
Whose glory and renown
Are spread o'er land and sea—
And wouldst thou hew it down?
Woodman, forbear thy stroke!
Cut not its earth-bound ties;
Oh, spare that aged oak
Now towering to the skies!

When but an idle boy,
I sought its grateful shade;
In all their gushing joy
Here, too, my sisters played.

Woodman, Spare That Tree!

My mother kissed me here;
My father pressed my hand—
Forgive this foolish tear,
But let that old oak stand.

My heartstrings round thee cling,
Close as thy bark, old friend!
Here shall the wild bird sing,
And still thy branches bend.
Old tree! the storm still brave!
And, woodman, leave the spot;
While I've a hand to save,
Thy ax shall harm it not.

George Pope Morris

BIRD
DAY

BIRD TRADES

*T*HE swallow is a mason,
  And underneath the eaves
He builds a nest and plasters it
  With mud and hay and leaves.

Of all the weavers that I know,
  The oriole is the best;
High on the branches of the tree
  She hangs her cosy nest.

The woodpecker is hard at work—
  A carpenter is he—
And you may hear him hammering,
  His nest high up a tree.

Some little birds are miners;
  Some build upon the ground;
And busy little tailors too,
  Among the birds are found.

Unknown

BIRDS IN SUMMER

*H*OW pleasant the life of a bird must be
  Flitting about in each leafy tree;
In the leafy trees so broad and tall,
Like a green and beautiful palace hall,
With its airy chambers, light and boon,
That open to sun, and stars, and moon;
That open unto the bright blue sky,
And the frolicsome winds as they wander by!

They have left their nests in the forest bough;
Those homes of delight they need not now;
And the young and old they wander out,
And traverse the green world round about;
And hark at the top of this leafy hall,
How, one to another, they lovingly call!
"Come up, come up!" they seem to say,
"Where the topmost twigs in the breezes play!"

"Come up, come up, for the world is fair,
Where the merry leaves dance in the summer
  air!"
And the birds below give back the cry,
"We come, we come to the branches high!"

Birds in Summer

How pleasant the life of the birds must be,
Living above in a leafy tree!
And away through the air what joy to go,
And to look on the green, bright earth below!

How pleasant the life of a bird must be,
Skimming about on the breezy sea,
Cresting the billows like silvery foam,
Then wheeling away to its cliff-built home!
What joy it must be to sail, upborne,
By a strong free wing, through the rosy morn,
To meet the young sun, face to face,
And pierce, like a shaft, the boundless space!

To pass through the bowers of the silver cloud;
To sing in the thunder halls aloud:
To spread out the wings for a wild, free flight
With the upper cloud-winds,—oh, what delight!
Oh, what would I give, like a bird, to go,
Right on through the arch of the sun-lit bow,
And see how the water-drops are kissed
Into green and yellow and amethyst.

How pleasant the life of a bird must be,
Wherever it listeth, there to flee;
To go, when a joyful fancy calls,
Dashing down 'mong the waterfalls:

Child's Song in Spring

Then wheeling about, with its mate at play,
Above and below, and among the spray,
Hither and thither, with screams as wild
As the laughing mirth of a rosy child!

What joy it must be, like a living breeze,
To flutter about 'mid the flowering trees;
Lightly to soar and to see beneath,
The wastes of the blossoming purple heath,
And the yellow furze, like fields of gold,
That gladden some fairy region old!
On mountain-tops, on the billowy sea,
On the leafy stems of the forest-tree,
How pleasant the life of a bird must be!

Mary Howitt

CHILD'S SONG IN SPRING

*T*HE silver birch is a dainty lady,
   She wears a satin gown;
The elm tree makes the old churchyard shady,
   She will not live in town.

The English oak is a sturdy fellow,
   He gets his green coat late;

The willow is smart in a suit of yellow,
　While brown the beech trees wait.

Such a gay green gown God gives the larches—
　As green as He is good!
The hazels hold up their arms for arches
　When Spring rides through the wood.

The chestnut's proud, and the lilac's pretty,
　The poplar's gentle and tall,
But the plane tree's kind to the poor dull city—
　I love him best of all!

Edith Nesbit

ROBERT OF LINCOLN

*M*ERRILY swinging on brier and weed,
　　Near to the nest of his little dame,
Over the mountain-side or mead,
　Robert of Lincoln is telling his name;
　　　Bob-o'-link, bob-o'-link,
　　　Spink, spank, spink;
Snug and safe is that nest of ours,
Hidden among the summer flowers,
　　　Chee, chee, chee.

Robert of Lincoln

Robert of Lincoln is gayly drest,
 Wearing a bright black wedding-coat;
White are his shoulders and white his crest.
 Hear him call in his merry note:
  Bob-o'-link, bob-o'-link,
  Spink, spank, spink;
Look, what a nice new coat is mine,
Sure there never was bird so fine.
  Chee, chee, chee.

Robert of Lincoln's Quaker wife,
 Pretty and quiet, with plain brown wings,
Passing at home a patient life,
 Broods in the grass while her husband sings
  Bob-o'-link, bob-o'-link,
  Spink, spank, spink;
Brood, kind creature, you need not fear
Thieves and robbers while I am here.
  Chee, chee, chee.

Modest and shy as a nun is she;
 One weak chirp is her only note.
Braggart and prince of braggarts is he,
 Pouring boasts from his little throat;
  Bob-o'-link, bob-o'-link,
  Spink, spank, spink;

Robert of Lincoln

Never was I afraid of man;
Catch me, cowardly knaves, if you can!
      Chee, chee, chee.

Six white eggs on a bed of hay,
    Flecked with purple, a pretty sight!
There, as the mother sits all day,
    Robert is singing with all his might:
        Bob-o'-link, bob-o'-link,
        Spink, spank, spink;
Nice good wife, that never goes out,
Keeping house while I frolic about.
      Chee, chee, chee.

Soon as the little ones chip the shell,
    Six wide mouths are open for food;
Robert of Lincoln bestirs him well,
    Gathering seeds for the hungry brood.
        Bob-o'-link, bob-o'-link,
        Spink, spank, spink;
This new life is likely to be
Hard for a gay young fellow like me.
      Chee, chee, chee.

Robert of Lincoln at length is made
    Sober with work and silent with care;

Off is his holiday garment laid,
Half forgotten that merry air;
    Bob-o'-link, bob-o'-link,
    Spink, spank, spink;
Nobody knows but my mate and I
Where our nest and our nestlings lie.
    Chee, chee, chee.

Summer wanes; the children are grown;
    Fun and frolic no more he knows;
Robert of Lincoln's a humdrum crone;
    Off he flies, and we sing as he goes:
        Bob-o'-link, bob-o'-link,
        Spink, spank, spink;
When you can pipe that merry old strain,
Robert of Lincoln, come back again.
        Chee, chee, chee.

William Cullen Bryant

THREE O'CLOCK IN THE MORNING

*W*HAT do the robins whisper about
        From their homes in the elms and
    birches?
I've tried to study the riddle out,
But still in my mind is many a doubt,
    In spite of deep researches.

Three o'Clock in the Morning

While all the world is in silence deep,
    In the twilight of early dawning,
They begin to chirp and twitter and peep,
As if they were talking in their sleep,
    At three o'clock in the morning.

Perhaps they tell secrets that should not be
    heard
    By mortals listening and prying;
Perhaps we might learn from some whispered
    word
The best way to bring up a little bird,
    Or the wonderful art of flying.

It may be the gossip from nest to nest,
    Hidden and leaf-enfolded;
For do we not often hear it confessed,
When a long-kept secret at last is guessed,
    That "a little bird has told it"?

What do the robins whisper about
    In the twilight of early dawning?
Listen, and tell me, if you find it out,
What 'tis the robins whisper about
    At three o'clock in the morning.

Unknown

TO A SKYLARK

*H*AIL to thee, blithe spirit!
    Bird thou never wert,
That from heaven, or near it,
    Pourest thy full heart
In profuse strains of unpremeditated art.

Higher still and higher
    From the earth thou springest
Like a cloud of fire;
    The blue deep thou wingest,
And singing still dost soar, and soaring ever
        singest.

In the golden lightning
    Of the sunken sun,
O'er which clouds are brightening,
    Thou dost float and run,
Like an unbodied joy whose race is just begun.

The pale purple even
    Melts around thy flight;
Like a star of heaven,

To a Skylark

In the broad daylight
Thou art unseen, but yet I hear thy shrill
delight.

All the earth and air
With thy voice is loud,
As, when night is bare,
From one lonely cloud
The moon rains out her beams, and heaven is
overflowed.

Sound of vernal showers
On the twinkling grass,
Rain-awakened flowers,
All that ever was
Joyous, and clear, and fresh, thy music doth
surpass.

Teach us, sprite or bird,
What sweet thoughts are thine:
I have never heard
Praise of love or wine
That painted forth a flood of rapture so divine

Chorus hymeneal
Or triumphal chant

Matched with thine would be all
    But an empty vaunt—
A thing wherein we feel there is some hidden
    want.

    *   *   *   *   *   *   *

Teach me half the gladness
    That thy brain must know,
Such harmonious madness
    From my lips would flow,
The world should listen then, as I am listening
    now!

Percy Bysshe Shelley

WHAT DOES LITTLE BIRDIE SAY?

*W*HAT does little birdie say?
    In her nest at peep of day?
"Let me fly," says little birdie,
    "Mother, let me fly away."

Birdie, rest a little longer,
Till the little wings are stronger,
So she rests a little longer,
    Then she flies away.

What Does Little Birdie Say?

What does little baby say,
In her bed at peep of day?
Baby says, like little birdie,
  "Let me rise and fly away."

Baby, sleep a little longer,
Till the little limbs are stronger.
If she sleeps a little longer,
  Baby, too, shall fly away.

Alfred, Lord Tennyson

EASTER

AT EASTER TIME

*T*HE little flowers came through the ground,
　　At Easter time, at Easter time:
They raised their heads and looked around,
　　At happy Easter time.
And every pretty bud did say,
　"Good people, bless this holy day,
For Christ is risen, the angels say
　　At happy Easter time!"

The pure white lily raised its cup
　　At Easter time, at Easter time.
The crocus to the sky looked up
　　At happy Easter time.
"We'll hear the song of Heaven!" they say,
　　"Its glory shines on us to-day.
Oh! may it shine on us alway.
　　At holy Easter time!"

'Twas long and long and long ago,
　　That Easter time, that Easter time:
But still the pure white lilies blow
　　At happy Easter time.

[97]

And still each little flower doth say
  "Good Christians, bless this holy day,
For Christ is risen, the angels say
  At blessed Easter time!"

Laura E. Richards

THE DAY OF JOY

*T*HIS is the gladness of our Easter morning—
  That nothing now in all the world is dead,
The roadside dust is tinted with forewarning
  Of heavenly verdure mortal feet shall tread.
New meanings each blue break of sky discloses;
  New messages on all the winds are heard;
New fragrance haunts the lilies and the roses—
  His life, His breath—the Spirit and the word.

The flowers of spring are no vain decoration
  Of earth's dead bosom; earth is all alive
In the awakening dawn of new creation,
    Whence soul and body perfect strength
    derive.
The untainted health, the everlasting beauty!
  Even frozen hearts the warm contagion feel
Of spiritual love and holy duty;

The sickliest plant Christ's living touch can
　heal.

This is the wonder of the Resurrection—
　That things unvalued now reveal their worth
That every human longing and affection
　Feels now the glow of its immortal birth.
Our common toil, the mutual hopes we cherish,
　The friendly word, the homely help we give
Each other in His love's name, shall not perish;
　No thought that lives in him shall cease to
　live.

We who are of the earth need not be earthly;
　God made our nature like His own, divine;
Nothing but selfishness can be unworthy
　Of His pure image meant through us to shine.
The death of deaths it is, ourself to smother
　In our own pleasures, His dishonored gift;
And life—eternal life—to love each other;
　Our souls with Christ in sacrifice to lift.

This is the beauty of our Easter morning;
　In Him humanity may now arise
Out of the grave of self, all baseness scorning—
　The holy radiance of His glorious eyes

Illumines everywhere uplifted faces;
  Touches the earthly with a heavenly glow;
And in that blessed light all human graces
  Unto divine beatitudes must grow.

Feeding on husks no more, the wanderers gather
  Around the hearthstone of the house above—
The Son has brought them home unto the
    Father;
  His spirit in their hearts is peace and love.
Souls speak in the lost language of communion,
  And angels echo back the words they say,
Earth is restored to heaven in deathless union—
  This is the glory of our Easter day.

Lucy Larcom

EASTER

*O*N Easter morn
    Up the faint cloudy sky
I hear the Easter bell,
Ding dong . . . ding dong . . .
Easter morning scatters lilies
On every doorstep;
Easter morning says a glad thing

Over and over.
Poor people, beggars, old women
Are hearing the Easter bell . . .
Ding dong . . . ding dong . . .

Hilda Conkling

EASTER

*T*HE barrier stone has rolled away,
   And loud the angels sing;
The Christ comes forth this blessed day
   To reign, a deathless king.
For shall we not believe He lives
   Through such awakening?
Behold, how God each April gives
   The miracle of Spring.

Edwin L. Sabin

AN EASTER CAROL

*S*PRING bursts to-day,
   For Christ is risen and all the earth's at
play.

   Flash forth, thou Sun.
The rain is over and gone, its work is done.
[101]

An Easter Carol

Winter is past,
Sweet Spring is come at last, is come at last.

Bud, Fig and Vine,
Bud, Olive, far with fruit and oil and wine.

Break forth this morn
In roses, thou but yesterday a thorn.

Uplift thy head,
O pure white Lily through the Winter dead.

Beside your dams
Leap and rejoice, you merry-making Lambs.

All Herds and Flocks
Rejoice, all Beasts of thickets and of rocks.

Sing, Creatures, sing,
Angels and Men and Birds and everything.

Christina G. Rossetti

EASTER HYMN

*A*WAKE, thou wintry earth,
   Fling off thy sadness!
Fair, vernal flowers, laugh forth
   Your ancient gladness!
      Christ is risen!

Warm, woods, your blossoms all,
   Grim Death is dead!
Ye weeping, funeral trees,
   Lift up your head:
      Christ is risen!

Come, see! the graves are green;
   It is light, let us go
Where our loved ones rest
   In hope below:
      Christ is risen!

All is fresh and new
   Full of Spring and light.
Wintry heart, why wear'st the hue
   Of sleep and night?
      Christ is risen!

[103]

Easter Hymn

Leave thy cares beneath,
   Leave thy worldly love!
Begin the better life
   With God above.
         Christ is risen!

                    Thomas Blackburn

EASTER HYMN

CHRIST the Lord is risen to-day,
   Sons of men and angels say:
Raise your joys and triumphs high,
Sing, ye heavens, and earth reply.

Love's redeeming work is done,
Fought the fight, the battle won:
Lo! our Sun's eclipse is o'er;
Lo! He sets in blood no more.

Vain the stone, the watch, the seal;
Christ hath burst the gates of Hell!
Death in vain forbids His rise;
Christ hath opened Paradise!

Easter Music

Lives again our glorious King:
Where, O Death, is now thy sting?
Once He died, our souls to save:
Where thy victory, O Grave?

Charles Wesley

EASTER MUSIC

*B*LOW, golden trumpets, sweet and clear,
  Blow soft upon the perfumed air;
    Bid the sad earth to join your song,
      "To Christ does victory belong!"

Oh, let the winds your message bear
To every heart of grief and care;
    Sound through the world the joyful lay,
      "Our Christ has conquered Death to-day!"

On cloudy wings let glad words fly
Through the soft blue of echoing sky:
    Ring out, O trumpets, sweet and clear.
      "Through Death immortal Life is here!"

Margaret Deland

SONG OF EASTER

SING, children, sing!
   And the lily censers swing;
Sing that life and joy are waking and that Death
      no more is king.
Sing the happy, happy tumult of the slowly
      brightening spring;
   Sing, children, sing!

   Sing, children, sing!
Winter wild has taken wing.
Fill the air with the sweet tiding till the frosty
      echoes ring!
Along the eaves the icicles no longer glittering
      cling:
And the crocus in the garden lifts its bright face
      to the Sun,
And in the meadows softly the brooks begin to
      run;
And the golden catkins swing
In the warm airs of the spring;
   Sing, little children, sing!

Celia Thaxter

[106]

MAY
DAY

AS WE DANCE ROUND

*A*S we dance round a-ring-a-ring,
  A maiden goes a-maying;
And here a flower, and there a flower,
Through mead and meadow straying;
O gentle one, why dost thou weep?—
Silver to spend with; gold to keep;
Till spin the green round World asleep,
And Heaven its dews be staying.

Unknown

THE COMING OF SPRING

*T*HERE'S something in the air
  That's new and sweet and rare—
A scent of summer things,
A whir as if of wings.

There's something, too, that's new
In the color of the blue
That's in the morning sky,
Before the sun is high.

And though on plain and hill
'Tis winter, winter still,

The Coming of Spring

There's something seems to say
That winter's had its day.

And all this changing tint,
This whispering stir and hint
Of bud and bloom and wing,
Is the coming of the spring.

And to-morrow or to-day
The brooks will break away
From their icy, frozen sleep,
And run, and laugh, and leap.

And the next thing, in the woods,
The catkins in their hoods
Of fur and silk will stand,
A sturdy little band.

And the tassels soft and fine
Of the hazel will entwine,
And the elder branches show
Their buds against the snow.

So, silently but swift,
Above the wintry drift,
The long days gain and gain,
Until on hill and plain,—

The Elves' Dance

Once more, and yet once more,
Returning as before,
We see the bloom of birth
Make young again the earth.

Nora Perl

THE ELVES' DANCE

ROUND about, round about
        In a fair ring-a,
Thus we dance, thus we dance
And thus we sing-a,
Trip and go, to and fro
Over this green-a,
All about, in and out,
For our brave Queen-a.

Unknown

HERE WE COME A–PIPING

HERE we come a-piping,
        In Springtime and in May;
Green fruit a-ripening,
And Winter fled away.
The Queen she sits upon the strand,

[111]

The Little Plant

Fair as lily, white as wand;
Seven billows on the sea,
Horses riding fast and free,
And bells beyond the sand.

Unknown

THE LITTLE PLANT

*I*N the heart of a seed
  Buried deep, so deep,
A dear little plant
  Lay fast asleep.

"Wake!" said the sunshine
  "And creep to the light,"
"Wake!" said the voice
  Of the raindrops bright.

The little plant heard,
  And it rose to see
What the wonderful
  Outside world might be.

Kate L. Brown

MAY SONG

$\mathcal{S}$PRING is coming, spring is coming,
    Birdies, build your nest;
Weave together straw and feather,
    Doing each your best.

Spring is coming, spring is coming,
    Flowers are coming too:
Pansies, lilies, daffodillies,
    Now are coming through.

Spring is coming, spring is coming,
    All around is fair;
Shimmer and quiver on the river,
    Joy is everywhere.

Old English Country Rime

OLD MAY SONG

$\mathcal{A}$LL in this pleasant evening, together come
    are we,
For the summer springs so fresh, green, and gay;
We tell you of a blossoming and buds on every
    tree,
Drawing near unto the merry month of May.

[113]

Old May Song

Rise up, the master of this house, put on your
    charm of gold,
For the summer springs so fresh, green, and gay;
Be not in pride offended with your name we
    make so bold,
Drawing near unto the merry month of May.

Rise up, the mistress of this house, with gold
    along your breast;
For the summer springs so fresh, green, and gay;
And if your body be asleep, we hope your soul's
    at rest,
Drawing near unto the merry month of May.

Rise up, the children of this house, all in your
    rich attire,
For the summer springs so fresh, green, and gay;
And every hair upon your heads shines like the
    silver wire;
Drawing near unto the merry month of May.

God bless this house and arbour, your riches and
    your store,
For the summer springs so fresh, green, and gay:

Spring

We hope the Lord will prosper you, both now
  and evermore,
Drawing near unto the merry month of May.

And now comes we must leave you, in peace and
  plenty here,
For the summer springs so fresh, green, and gay;
We shall not sing you May again until another
  year,
To draw you these cold winters away.

Unknown

SPRING

*T*HE alder by the river
    Shakes out her powdery curls;
The willow buds in silver
    For little boys and girls.

The little birds fly over,
    And oh, how sweet they sing!
To tell the happy children
    That once again 'tis spring.

The gay green grass comes creeping
    So soft beneath their feet;

Spring Song

The frogs begin to ripple
A music clear and sweet.

And buttercups are coming,
And scarlet columbine;
And in the sunny meadows
The dandelions shine.

And just as many daisies
As their soft hands can hold
The little ones may gather,
All fair in white and gold.

Here blows the warm red clover,
There peeps the violet blue;
O happy little children,
God made them all for you!

Celia Thaxter

SPRING SONG

I LOVE daffodils.
I love Narcissus when he bends his head.
I can hardly keep March and Spring and Sunday
and daffodils
Out of my rhyme of song.

Spring Song

Do you know anything about the spring
When it comes again?
God knows about it while winter is lasting.
Flowers bring him power in the spring,
And birds bring it, and children.
He is sometimes sad and alone
Up there in the sky trying to keep his worlds
  happy.
I bring him songs
When he is in his sadness and weary.
I tell him how I used to wander out
To study stars and the moon he made,
And flowers in the dark of the wood.
I keep reminding him about his flowers he has
  forgotten,
And that snowdrops are up.
What can I say to make him listen?
"God," I say,
"Don't you care.
Nobody must be sad or sorry
In the spring-time of flowers."

Hilda Conkling

WHO CALLS?

*L*ISTEN, children, listen, won't you come
    into the night?
The stars have set their candle gleam, the moon
    her lantern light.
I'm piping little tunes for you to catch your
    dancing feet.
There's glory in the heavens, but there's magic
    in the street.

There's jesting here and carnival: the cost of
    a balloon
Is an ancient rhyme said backwards, and a
    wish upon the moon.
The city walls and· city streets!—you shall
    make of these
As fair a thing as country roads and blossomy
    apple trees."

"What watchman calls us in the night, and plays
    a little tune
That turns our tongues to talking now of April,
    May and June?
Who bids us come with nimble feet and snap-
    ping finger tips?"
"I am the Spring, the Spring, the Spring with
    laughter on my lips."   *Frances Clarke*

MOTHER'S
DAY

A BOY'S MOTHER

MY mother she's so good to me,
    Ef I was good as I could be,
I couldn't be as good—no, sir.—
Can't any boy be good as her.

She loves me when I'm glad er sad;
She loves me when I'm good er bad;
An', what's a funniest thing, she says
She loves me when she punishes.

I don't like her to punish me,—
That don't hurt—but it hurts to see
Her cryin'.—Nen I cry; an' nen
We both cry an' be good again.

She loves me when she cuts an' sews
My little cloak an' Sund'y clothes;
An' when my Pa comes home to tea,
She loves him most as much as me.

She laughs an' tells him all I said,
An' grabs me up an' pats my head;
An' I hug her, an' hug my Pa,
An' love him purt' nigh as much as Ma.

James Whitcomb Riley

CHILD AND MOTHER

O MOTHER-MY-LOVE, if you'll give me
  your hand,
 And go where I ask you to wander,
I will lead you away to a beautiful land—
 The Dreamland that's waiting out yonder.
We'll walk in a sweet-posie garden out there
 Where moonlight and starlight are streaming
And the flowers and birds are filling the air
 With fragrance and music of dreaming.

There'll be no little tired-out boy to undress,
 No questions or cares to perplex you;
There'll be no little bruises or bumps to caress,
 Nor patching of stockings to vex you.
For I'll rock you away on a silver-dew stream,
 And sing you asleep when you're weary,
And no one shall know of our beautiful dream
 But you and your own little dearie.

[122]

For You, Mother

And when I am tired I'll nestle my head
  In the bosom that's soothed me so often
And the wide-awake stars shall sing in my
  stead
  A song which our dreaming shall soften.
So Mother-my-Love, let me take your dear
  hand,
  And away through the starlight we'll
  wander—
Away through the mist to the beautiful land—
  The Dreamland that's waiting out yonder!

Eugene Field

FOR YOU, MOTHER

I HAVE a dream for you, Mother,
  Like a soft thick fringe to hide your eyes.
I have a surprise for you, Mother,
Shaped like a strange butterfly.
I have found a way of thinking
To make you happy;
I have made a song and a poem
All twisted into one.
If I sing, you listen;
If I think, you know

[123]

Grown-ups

I have a secret from everybody in the world
    full of people
But I cannot always remember how it goes;
It is a song
For you, Mother,
With a curl of cloud and a feather of blue
And a mist
Blowing along the sky.
If I sing it some day, under my voice,
Will it make you happy?

Hilda Conkling

GROWN-UPS

AUNTIES know all about fairies,
    Uncles know all about guns,
Mothers and fathers think all the day long
Of making their children happy and strong,
    Even the little ones.

Rose Fyleman

THE LITTLE GIRL THAT MOTHER USED TO BE

*W*HEN we travel back in summer to the old
    house by the sea,
Where long ago my mother lived, a little girl
    like me,
I have the strangest notion that she still is wait-
    ing there,
A small child in a pinafore with ribbon on her
    hair.
I hear her in the garden when I go to pick a rose;
She follows me along the path on dancing tipsy
    toes;
I hear her in the hayloft when the hay is
    slippery—sweet—
A rustle and a scurry and a sound of scamper-
    ing feet;
Yet though I sit as still as still, she never comes
    to me,
The funny little laughing girl my mother used
    to be.
Sometimes I nearly catch her as she dodges
    here and there,

Mother

Her white dress flutters round a tree and flashes
    up a stair;
Sometimes I almost put my hand upon her
    apron strings—
Then, just before my fingers close, she's gone
    again like wings.
A sudden laugh, a scrap of song, a footfall on
    the lawn,
And yet, no matter how I run, forever up and
    gone!
A fairy or a firefly could hardly flit so fast.
When we come home in summer, I have given
    up at last.
I lay my cheek on mother's.   If there's only one
    for me,
I'd rather have her, anyway, than the girl she
    used to be.

Nancy Byrd Turner

MOTHER

*W*HEN mother comes each morning
    She wears her oldest things,
She doesn't make a rustle,
    She hasn't any rings;
[126]

Mother

She says, "Good morning, chickies,
　　It's such a lovely day,
Let's go into the garden
　　And have a game of play:"

When mother comes at tea-time
　　Her dress goes shoo-shoo-shoo,
She always has a little bag,
　　Sometimes a sunshade too;
She says, "I am so hoping
　　There's something left for me;
Please hurry up, dear Nanna,
　　I'm dying for my tea."

When mother comes at bed-time
　　Her evening dress she wears,
She tells us each a story
　　When we have said our prayers;
And if there is a party
　　She looks so shiny bright
It's like a lovely fairy
　　Dropped in to say good-night.

Rose Fyleman

OUR MOTHER

*H*UNDREDS of stars in the pretty sky,
   Hundreds of shells on the shore together,
Hundreds of birds that go singing by,
Hundreds of birds in the sunny weather.
Hundreds of dew-drops to greet the dawn,
Hundreds of bees in the purple clover,
Hundreds of butterflies on the lawn,
But only one Mother the wide world over.

Unknown

SONGS FOR MY MOTHER

I

Her Hands

*M*Y mother's hands are cool and fair,
   They can do anything.
Delicate mercies hide them there
   Like flowers in the spring.

Songs for My Mother

When I was small and could not sleep,
   She used to come to me,
And with my cheek upon her hand
   How sure my rest would be.

For everything she ever touched
   Of beautiful or fine,
Their memories living in her hands
   Would warm that sleep of mine.

Her hands remember how they played
   One time in meadow streams,—
And all the flickering song and shade
   Of water took my dreams.

Swift through her haunted fingers pass
   Memories of garden things;—
I dipped my face in flowers and grass
   And sounds of hidden wings.

One time she touched the cloud that kissed
   Brown pastures bleak and far;—
I leaned my cheek into a mist
   And thought I was a star.

[129]

Songs for My Mother

All this was very long ago
    And I am grown; but yet
The hand that lured my slumber so
    I never can forget.

For still when drowsiness comes on
    It seems so soft and cool,
Shaped happily beneath my cheek,
    Hollow and beautiful.

II

Her Words

My mother has the prettiest tricks
    Of words and words and words.
Her talk comes out as smooth and sleek
    As breasts of singing birds.

She shapes her speech all silver fine
    Because she loves it so.
And her own eyes begin to shine
    To hear her stories grow.

And if she goes to make a call
    Or out to take a walk
We leave our work when she returns
    And run to hear her talk.

We had not dreamed these things were so
    Of sorrow and of mirth.
Her speech is as a thousand eyes
    Through which we see the earth.

God wove a web of loveliness,
    Of clouds and stars and birds,
But made not anything at all
    So beautiful as words.

They shine around our simple earth
    With golden shadowings,
And every common thing they touch
    Is exquisite with wings.

There's nothing poor and nothing small
    But is made fair with them.
They are the hands of living faith
    That touch the garment's hem.

They are as fair as bloom or air,
 They shine like any star,
And I am rich who learned from her
 How beautiful they are.

Anna Hempstead Branch

WHICH LOVED HER BEST?

I LOVE you, mother," said little John;
 Then, forgetting his work, his cap went on,
And he was off to the garden swing,
Leaving his mother the wood to bring.

"I love you, mother," said rosy Nell;
"I love you better than tongue can tell;"
Then she teased and pouted full half the day,
Till her mother rejoiced when she went to play.

"I love you, mother," said little Fan;
"To-day I'll help you all I can;
How glad I am that school doesn't keep!"
So she rocked the baby till it fell asleep.

Which Loved Her Best?

Then, stepping softly, she took the broom,
And swept the floor, and dusted the room;
Busy and happy all day was she,
Helpful and cheerful as child could be.

"I love you, mother," again they said—
Three little children going to bed;
How do you think that mother guessed
Which of them really loved her best?

Joy Allison

MUSIC
WEEK

THE AIM WAS SONG

*B*EFORE man came to blow it right
   The wind once blew itself untaught,
And did its loudest day and night
   In any rough place where it caught.

Man came to tell it what was wrong:
   It hadn't found the place to blow;
It blew too hard—the aim was song,
   And listen—how it ought to go!

He took a little in his mouth,
   And held it long enough for north
To be converted into south
   And then by measure blew it forth.

By measure. It was word and note,
   The way the wind had meant to be—
A little through the lips and throat.
   The aim was song—the wind could see.

Robert Frost

[137]

FAIRY MUSIC

*W*HEN the fiddlers play their tunes you may
    sometimes hear,
Very softly chiming in, magically clear,
Magically high and sweet, the tiny crystal notes
Of fairy voices bubbling free from tiny fairy
    throats.

When birds at break of day chant their morning
    prayers,
Or on sunny afternoons pipe ecstatic airs,
Comes an added rush of sound to the silver
    din—
Songs of fairy troubadours gaily joining in.

When athwart the drowsy fields summer twilight
    falls,
Through the tranquil air there float elfin mad-
    rigals,
And in wild November nights, on the winds
    astride,
Fairy hosts go rushing by, singing as they ride.

Every dream that mortals dream, sleeping or
    awake,
Every lovely fragile hope—these the fairies
    take,
Delicately fashion them and give them back
    again
In tender, limpid melodies that charm the
    hearts of men.

Rose Fyleman

LEARNING TO PLAY

*U*PON a tall piano stool
    I have to sit and play
A stupid finger exercise
    For half an hour a day.

They call it "playing," but to me
    It's not a bit of fun.
I play when I am out of doors,
    Where I can jump and run.

But Mother says the little birds
    Who sing so nicely now,
Had first to learn, and practice too,
    All sitting on a bough.

And maybe if I practice hard,
　　Like them, I too, some day,
Shall make the pretty music sound;
　　Then I shall call it "play."

Abbie Farwell Brown

MUSIC

*I*F I think music,
　　It comes and goes.
If the fountain ripples and splashes,
It keeps on singing.
Falling broken water
Sings and answers
When the warblers in the May trees
Stay close for a little.
But music that I hear
Is different in its meanings. . . .
Happy hour or sorrowing
Into change.

Hilda Conkling

MUSIC

*W*HEN music sounds, gone is the earth I know,
And all her lovely things even lovelier grow;

Her flowers in vision flame, her forest-trees
Lift burdened branches, stilled with ecstasies.

When music sounds, out of the water rise
Naiads whose beauty dims my waking eyes,
Rapt in strange dreams burns each enchanted
    face,
With solemn echoing stirs their dwelling place.

When music sounds, all that I was I am
Ere to this haunt of brooding dust I came;
While from Time's woods break into distant
    song
The swift-winged hours, as I haste along.

Walter de la Mare

MUSIC'S SILVER SOUND

*W*HEN gripping grief the heart doth wound,
    And doleful dumps the mind oppress,
Then music, with her silver sound,
    With speedy help doth lend redress.

William Shakespeare

THE WORLD'S MUSIC

*T*HE world's a very happy place,
  Where every child should dance and sing
And always have a smiling face,
  And never sulk for anything.

I waken when the morning's come,
  And feel the air and light alive
With strange sweet music like the hum
  Of bees about their busy hive.

The linnets play among the leaves
  At hide-and-seek, and chirp and sing;
While, flashing to and from the eaves,
  The swallows twitter on the wing.

And twigs that shake, and boughs that sway;
  And tall old trees you cannot climb;
And winds that come, but cannot stay,
  Are singing gayly all the time.

From dawn to dark the old mill-wheel
  Makes music, going round and round;
And dusty-white with flour and meal,
  The miller whistles to its sound.

The World's Music

The brook that flows beside the mill,
  As happy as a brook can be,
Goes singing its old song until
  It learns the singing of the sea.

For every wave upon the sands
  Sings songs you never tire to hear,
Of laden ships from sunny lands
  Where it is summer all the year.

And if you listen to the rain
  Where leaves and birds and bees are dumb,
You hear it pattering on the pane
  Like Andrew beating on his drum.

The coals beneath the kettle croon,
  And clap their hands and dance in glee;
And even the kettle hums a tune
  To tell you when its time for tea.

The world is such a happy place
  That children, whether big or small,
Should always have a smiling face
  And never, never sulk at all.

Gabriel Setoun

MEMORIAL DAY

BENEATH THE FLAG

ON the sunny hillside sleeping,
    On the calm and placid plain,
By the rivers swiftly sweeping,
    By the rudely roaring main,
Lie the men who saved the nation
    In the dark hour long ago,
Meeting death with proud elation
    From a brave but erring foe.

In their earthly sleep unending
    Do the nation's martyred sons
Hear the war shouts hoarsely blending
    With the booming of the guns?
Do they quicken at the rattle
    As the mighty band sweeps by?
Do they see that still in battle
    Heroes rise to do or die?

Let us hope these warriors knighted
    In the bright hereafter know
That our nation firm united
    Faces now a common foe;

That beneath the dear Old Glory,
   Clearing freedom's splendid way,
Adding luster to its story,
   Side by side march Blue and Gray!

Cleveland Plain Dealer

THE BIVOUAC OF THE DEAD

*T*HE muffled drum's sad roll has beat
   The soldier's last tattoo;
No more on Life's parade shall meet
   That brave and fallen few.
On Fame's eternal camping-ground
   Their silent tents are spread,
And Glory guards, with solemn round,
   The bivouac of the dead.

No rumor of the foe's advance
   Now swells upon the wind;
No troubled thought at midnight haunts
   Of loved ones left behind;
No vision of the morrow's strife
   The warrior's dream alarms;
No braying horn nor screaming fife
   At dawn shall call to arms.

[148]

The Bivouac of the Dead

Their shivered swords are red with rust,
  Their plumèd heads are bowed;
Their haughty banner, trailed in dust,
  Is now their martial shroud.
And plenteous funeral tears have washed
  The red stains from each brow,
And the proud forms, by battle gashed,
  Are free from anguish now.

The neighing troop, the flashing blade,
  The bugle's stirring blast,
The charge, the dreadful cannonade,
  The din and shout, are past;
Nor war's wild note nor glory's peal
  Shall thrill with fierce delight
Those breasts that nevermore may feel
  The rapture of the fight.

*   *   *   *   *   *   *

Rest on, embalmed and sainted dead!
  Dear as the blood ye gave;
No impious footsteps here shall tread
  The herbage of your grave;
Nor shall your Glory be forgot
  While Fame her record keeps,
Or Honor points the hallowed spot
  Where Valor proudly sleeps.

Yon marble minstrel's voiceless stone
 In deathless song shall tell,
When many a vanished age hath flown,
 The story how ye fell;
Nor wreck, nor change, nor winter's blight,
 Nor Time's remorseless doom,
Shall dim one ray of glory's light
 That gilds your deathless tomb.

Theodore O'Hara

THE BLUE AND THE GRAY

*B*Y the flow of the inland river,
 Whence the fleets of iron have fled,
Where the blades of the grave-grass quiver,
 Asleep are the ranks of the dead;
Under the sod and the dew,
 Waiting the judgment day;
Under the one, the Blue,
 Under the other, the Gray.

These in the robings of glory,
 Those in the gloom of defeat,
All with the battle-blood gory,
 In the dusk of eternity meet;

[150]

The Blue and the Gray

Under the sod and the dew,
  Waiting the judgment day;
Under the laurel, the Blue,
  Under the willow, the Gray.

From the silence of sorrowful hours
  The desolate mourners go,
Lovingly laden with flowers
  Alike for the friend and the foe;
    Under the sod and the dew,
      Waiting the judgment day;
    Under the roses, the Blue,
      Under the lilies, the Gray.

  *   *   *   *   *   *

Sadly, but not with upbraiding,
  The generous deed was done,
In the storm of the years that are fading,
  No braver battle was won;
    Under the sod and the dew,
      Waiting the judgment day;
    Under the blossoms, the Blue,
      Under the garlands, the Gray.

No more shall the war-cry sever,
  Or the winding rivers be red;
They banish our anger forever
  When they laurel the graves of our dead!
    Under the sod and the dew,
      Waiting the judgment day;
    Love and tears for the Blue,
      Tears and love for the Gray.

Francis M. Finch

DECORATION DAY

SLEEP, comrades! sleep and rest
  On this field of grounded arms,
Where foes no more molest,
  Nor sentry's shot alarms.

Ye have slept on the ground before,
  And started to your feet
At the cannon's sudden roar,
  Or the drum's redoubling beat.

But in this camp of death
  No sound your slumber breaks;
Here is no fevered breath,
  No wound that bleeds and aches.

[152]

For Our Dead

All is repose and peace;
   Untrampled lies the sod;
The shouts of battle cease,—
   It is the Truce of God.

Rest, comrades! rest and sleep!
   The thoughts of men should be
As sentinels, to keep
   Your rest from dangers free.

Your silent tents of green
   We deck with fragrant flowers:
Yours has the suffering been,
   The memory shall be ours.

Henry Wadsworth Longfellow

FOR OUR DEAD

FLOWERS for our dead!
   The delicate wild roses, faintly red;
The valley lily beds, as purely white
As shines their honor in the vernal light;
All blooms that be
As fragrant as their fadeless memory!
By tender hands entwined and garlanded,
Flowers for our dead! . . .

Love for our dead!
O hearts that droop and mourn, be comforted!
The darksome path through the abyss of pain,
The final hour of travail not in vain!
For freedom's morning smile
Broadens across the seas from isle to isle.
By reverent lips let this fond word be said:
Love for our dead!

Clinton Scollard

HOW SLEEP THE BRAVE

*H*OW sleep the Brave who sink to rest
　　By all their country's wishes blest!
When Spring, with dewy fingers cold,
Returns to deck their hallowed mold,
She there shall dress a sweeter sod
Than Fancy's feet have ever trod.

By fairy hands their knell is rung:
By forms unseen their dirge is sung:
There honor comes, a pilgrim gray,
To bless the turf that wraps their clay;
And Freedom shall awhile repair,
To dwell a weeping hermit there.

William Collins

MEMORIAL DAY

*G*ATHER the garlands rare to-day,
   Snow-white roses and roses red;
Gather the fairest flowers of May,
Heap them up on the graves of clay,
   Gladden the graves of the noble dead.

Pile them high as the soldiers were
   Piled on the field when they fought and fell;
They will rejoice in their new place there
To-day, as they walk where the fragrant air
   Is sweet with the scent of asphodel.

Many a time, I've heard it said,
   They fell so thick where the battles were,
Their hot blood rippled, and, running red,
Ran out like a rill from the drifted dead
   Staining the heath and the daisies there.

This day the friends of the soldiers keep,
   And they will keep it through all the years,
To the silent city where soldiers sleep
Will come with flowers, to watch and weep
   And water the garlands with their tears.

Cy Warman

[155]

MEMORIAL DAY

I

T WINE laurels to lay o'er the Blue and the
Gray, spread wreaths where our heroes
rest;
Let the song of the North echo back from the
South for the love that is truest and best!
Twine wreaths for the tombs of our Grant and
our Lee, one anthem for Jackson and Meade.
And the flag above you is the banner for me—
one people in name and in deed!

II

Clasp hands o'er the graves where our laurelled
ones lie—clasp hands o'er the Gray and the
Blue;
To-day we are brothers and bound by a tie that
the years shall but serve to renew;
By the side of the Northman who peacefully
sleeps where tropical odors are shed
A song of the South his companionship keeps—
one flag o'er the two heroes spread.

Memorial Day

III

Weave tokens of love for the heroes in blue,
    weave wreaths for the heroes in gray;
Clasp brotherly hands o'er the graves that are
    new—for the love that is ours to-day;
A trinity given to bless, to unite—three glorious
    records to keep,
And a kinship that never a grievance shall sever
    renewed where the brave are asleep!

IV

Spread flowers to-day o'er the Blue and the
    Gray—spread wreaths where our heroes rest;
Let the song of the North echo back from the
    South for the love that is truest and best!
Twine wreaths for the tombs of our Grant and
    our Lee, one hymn for your father and mine!
Oh, the flag you adore is the banner for me and
    its folds our dead brothers entwine.

Samuel Ellsworth Kiser

THE NEW MEMORIAL DAY

*O*H, the roses we plucked for the blue
    And the lilies we twined for the gray,
We have bound in a wreath,
And in silence beneath,
  Slumber our heroes to-day.

Over the new-turned sod
  The sons of our fathers stand,
And the fierce old fight
Slips out of sight
  In the clasp of a brother's hand.

For the old blood left a stain
  That the new has washed away,
And the sons of those
That have faced as foes
  Are marching together to-day.

Oh, the blood that our fathers gave!
  Oh, the tide of our mothers' tears!
And the flow of red,
And the tears they shed,
  Embittered a sea of years.

But the roses we plucked for the blue,
　　And the lilies we twined for the gray,
We have bound in a wreath,
And in glory beneath
　　Slumber our heroes to-day.

Albert Bigelow Paine

SOLDIER, REST

SOLDIER, rest! thy warfare o'er,
　　Sleep the sleep that knows not breaking;
Dream of battle-fields no more,
　　Days of danger, nights of waking,
In our isle's enchanted hall,
　　Hands unseen thy couch are strewing;
Fairy strains of music fall,
　　Every sense in slumber dewing.
Soldier, rest! thy warfare o'er,
Dream of fighting fields no more:
Sleep the sleep that knows not breaking,
Morn of toil, nor night of waking.

No rude sound shall reach thine ear,
　　Armor's clang, or war-steed's champing;
Trump nor pibroch summon here,
　　Mustering clan, or squadron tramping.

Song for Decoration Day

Yet the lark's shrill fife may come,
　　At the day-break, from the fallow,
And the bittern sound his drum,
　　Booming from the sedgy shallow.
Ruder sounds shall none be near,
Guards nor warders challenge here,
Here's no war-steed's neigh and champing,
Shouting clans, or squadrons stamping.

Sir Walter Scott

SONG FOR DECORATION DAY

BRING forth the flowers,
　　Sweet fragrant flowers,
Born in the sunshine
And sparkling with dew;
Here while we sing,
Gladly we bring
Offerings meet for the brave and true.
Daisies and buttercups, roses and lilies fair,
Dainty forget-me-nots, violets blue.

Bring forth the flowers, sweet fragrant flowers,
Offerings sweet for the brave and the true.

We Keep Memorial Day

Heap high the flowers,
Sweet-scented flowers,
Bright garlands strew o'er their graves every-
    where;
While just above,
The flag that we love
Still floats its stars and stripes on the air.
Flag of our Union, brave soldiers defend thee,
Lay down their lives for thy color so fair,
Heap high the flowers, sweet-scented flowers,
Bright garlands strew o'er their graves every-
    where.

Helen C. Bacon

WE KEEP MEMORIAL DAY

WHEN the May has culled her flowers for
    the summer waiting long,
And the breath of early roses woos the hedges
    into song,
Comes the throb of martial music and the ban-
    ners in the street,
And the marching of the millions bearing gar-
    lands fair and sweet—

We Keep Memorial Day

'Tis the Sabbath of the Nation, 'tis the floral
    feast of May!
        In remembrance of our heroes
        We keep Memorial Day.

They are sleeping in the valleys, they are sleep-
    ing 'neath the sea,
They are sleeping by the thousands till the royal
    reveille;
Let us know them, let us name them, let us honor
    one and all,
For they loved us and they saved us, springing
    at the bugle call;
Let us sound the song and cymbal, wreathe the
    immortelles and bay.
        In the fervor of thanksgiving
        We keep Memorial Day.

Kate Brownlee Sherwood

FLAG
DAY

THE AMERICAN FLAG

*W*HEN Freedom from her mountain height
   Unfurled her standard to the air,
She tore the azure robe of night,
   And set the stars of glory there.
She mingled with its gorgeous dyes
The milky baldric of the skies,
And striped its pure celestial white
With streakings of the morning light;
Then from his mansion in the sun
She called her eagle bearer down,
And gave into his mighty hand
The symbol of her chosen land.

Majestic monarch of the cloud,
   Who rear'st aloft thy regal form,
To hear the tempest trumpings loud
And see the lightning lances driven,
   When strive the warriors of the storm,
And rolls the thunder-drum of heaven,
Child of the sun! to thee 'tis given
   To guard the banner of the free,

To hover in the sulphur smoke,
To ward away the battle stroke,
And bid its blending shine afar,
Like rainbows on the cloud of war,
    The harbingers of victory!

Flag of the brave! thy folds shall fly,
The sign of hope and triumph high,
When speaks the signal trumpet tone,
And the long line comes gleaming on.
Ere yet the life-blood, warm and wet,
Has dimmed the glistening bayonet,
Each soldier eye shall brightly turn
To where thy sky-born glories burn,
And, as his springing steps advance,
Catch war and vengeance from the glance,
And when the cannon-mouthings loud
Heave in wild wreaths the battle shroud,
And gory sabers rise and fall
Like shoots of flame on midnight's pall,
    Then shall thy meteor glances glow,
And cowering foes shall shrink beneath
    Each gallant arm that strikes below
That lovely messenger of death.

The American Flag

Flag of the seas! on ocean wave
Thy stars shall glitter o'er the brave;
When death, careering on the gale,
Sweeps darkly round the bellied sail,
And frighted waves rush wildly back
Before the broadside's reeling rack,
Each dying wanderer of the sea
Shall look at once to heaven and thee,
And smile to see thy splendors fly
In triumph o'er his closing eye.

Flag of the free heart's hope and home!
    By angel hands to valor given;
Thy stars have lit the welkin dome,
    And all thy hues were born in heaven.
Forever float that standard sheet!
    Where breathes the foe but falls before us,
With Freedom's soil beneath our feet,
    And Freedom's banner streaming o'er us?

Joseph Rodman Drake

THE AMERICAN FLAG

*L*IFT it high, our glorious banner;
  Let it wave upon the breeze;
Freedom's starry emblem ever,
Lift it high o'er land and seas.

Many conflicts it has witnessed,
Many stories it could tell
Of the brave who fought around it,
Of the brave who 'neath it fell.

Scenes of woe and desolation,
Scenes of joy o'er vic'tries won;
Scenes of rest and peaceful union;
Freedom now for every one.

Lift the flag, then, high above us,
May it wave till time shall cease,
And its record for the future,
Be of happiness and peace!

Lena E. Fauld

THE FLAG

SPIRITS of patriots, hail in heaven again
  The flag for which ye fought and died,
Now that its field, washed clear of every stain,
  Floats out in honest pride!

Free blood flows through its scarlet veins once
    more,
  And brighter shine its silver bars;
A deeper blue God's ether never wore
  Amongst the golden stars.

See how our earthly constellation gleams;
  And backward, flash for flash, returns
Its heavenly sisters their immortal beams
  With light that fires and burns,—

That burns because a moving soul is there,
  A living force, a shaping will,
Whose law the fate-forecasting powers of air
  Acknowledge and fulfill.

At length the day, by prophets seen of old,
  Flames on the crimsoned battlefields;
Henceforth, O flag, no mortal bought and sold,
  Shall crouch beneath thy shade.

[169]

That shame has vanished in the darkened past,
    With all the wild chaotic wrongs
That held the struggling centuries shackled fast
    With fear's accursed thongs.

Therefore, O patriot fathers, in your eyes
    I brandish thus our banner pure;
Watch o'er us, bless us, from your peaceful
    skies,
    And make the issue sure!

George Henry Boker

THE FLAG

*W*HY do I love our flag? Ask why
    Flowers love the sunshine. Or, ask why
The needle turns with eager eye
Toward the great stars in northern sky.

I love Old Glory, for it waved
Where loyal hearts the Union saved.
I love it, since it shelters me
And all most dear, from sea to sea,
I love it, for it bravely flies
In freedom's cause, 'neath foreign skies.

[170]

The Flag

I love it for its blessèd cheer,
Its starry hopes and scorn of fear;
For good achieved and good to be
To us and to humanity.

It is the people's banner bright,
Forever guiding toward the light;
Foe of the tyrant, friend of right,
God give it leadership, and might!

Edward A. Horton

THE FLAG

LET it idly droop, or sway,
    To the wind's light will;
Furl its stars, or float in day;
    Flutter, or be still!
It has held its colors bright,
    Through the war smoke dun;
Spotless emblem of the Right,
    Whence success was won.

Let it droop in graceful rest
    For a passing hour—
Glory's banner, last and best;
    Freedom's freshest flower!

[171]

The Flag

Each red stripe has blazoned forth
   Gospels writ in blood;
Every star has sung the birth
   Of some deathless good.

Let it droop, but not too long!
   On the eager wind
Bid it wave, to shame the wrong;
   To inspire mankind
With a larger, human love;
   With a truth as true
As the heaven that broods above
   Its deep field of blue.

In the gathering hosts of hope,
   In the march of man,
Open for it place and scope,
   Bid it lead the van;
Till beneath the searching skies
   Martyr-blood be found,
Purer than our sacrifice,
   Crying from the ground:

Till a flag with some new light
   Out of Freedom's sky,
Kindles, through the gulfs of night,
   Holier blazonry.

The Flag Goes By

Let its glow the darkness drown!
   Give our banner sway,
Till its joyful stars go down,
   In undreamed-of day!

Lucy Larcom

THE FLAG GOES BY

*H*ATS off!
   Along the street there comes
A blare of bugles, a ruffle of drums,
A flash of color beneath the sky;
Hats off!
The flag is passing by!

Blue and crimson and white it shines,
Over the steel-tipped, ordered lines.
Hats off!
The colors before us fly;
But more than the flag is passing by.

Sea-fights and land-fights, grim and great,
Fought to make and to save the State:
Weary marches and sinking ships;
Cheers of victory on dying lips;

[173]

Days of plenty and years of peace;
March of a strong land's swift increase;
Equal justice, right and law,
Stately honor and reverent awe;
Sign of a nation, great and strong
To ward her people from foreign wrong;
Pride and glory and honor,—all
Live in the colors to stand or fall.

Hats off!
Along the street there comes
A blare of bugles, a ruffle of drums;
And loyal hearts are beating high:
Hats off!
The flag is passing by!

Henry Holcomb Bennett

FLAG O' MY LAND

*U*P to the breeze of the morning I fling you.
    Blending your folds with the dawn in
    the sky;
There let the people behold you, and bring you
    Love and devotion that never shall die.
        Proudly, agaze at your glory, I stand,
        Flag o' my land! flag o' my land!

[174]

Flag o' My Land

Standard most glorious! banner of beauty!
  Whither you beckon me there will I go,
Only to you, after God, is my duty;
  Unto no other allegiance I owe.
    Heart of me, soul of me, yours to command,
    Flag o' my land! flag o' my land!

Pine to palmetto and ocean to ocean,
  Though of strange nations we get our in·
    crease,
Here are your worshippers one in devotion,
  Whether the bugles blow battle or peace,
    Take us and make us your patriot band,
    Flag o' my land! flag o' my land!

Now to the breeze of the morning I give you,
  Ah! but the days when the staff will be bare!
Teach us to see you and love you and live you
  When the light fades and your folds are not
    there.
    Dwell in the hearts that are yours to com·
      mand,
    Flag o' my land! flag o' my land!

T. A. Daly

[175]

FLAG OF THE FREE

*L*OOK at the flag as it floats on high,
    Streaming aloft in the clear, blue sky,
Rippling, leaping, tugging away,
Gay as the sunshine, bright as the day,
Throbbing with life, where the world may see—
Flag of our country, flag of the free!
What do we see in the flag on high,
That we bare our heads as it passes by,
That we thrill with pride, and our hearts beat
    fast,
And we cheer and cheer as the flag goes past—
The flag that waves for you and me—
Flag of our country, flag of the free?

We see in the flag a nation's might.
The pledge of a safeguard day and night,
Of a watchful eye and a powerful arm
That guard the nation's homes from harm.
Of a strong defense on land and sea—
Flag of our country, flag of the free!
We see in the flag a union grand,
A brotherhood of heart and hand,

A pledge of love and a stirring call
To live our lives for the good of all—
Helpful and just and true to thee,
Flag of our country, flag of the free!

Flutter, dear flag, o'er the lands and the seas!
Fling out your stars and your stripes to the
   breeze,
Righting all wrongs, dispelling all fear,
Guarding the land that we cherish so dear,
And the God of our fathers, abiding with thee,
Will bless you and trust you, O flag of the free!

                    Walter Taylor Field

THE LITTLE FLAGS

*O*H, when you see them flying
   Beside the summer way—
The little flags they put in place
   Upon Memorial Day—
Remember each is crying
   A message straight to you—
A message straight to every lad
   Whose heart is clean and true.

My Country's Flag

They tell the splendid story
  Of those who marched away
In answer to a voice that said,
  "Your country calls! Obey!"
They heard the call to glory,
  As you can, if you try:
"Your flag demands your best to-day,
  Not sometime, by and by!"

John Clair Minot

MY COUNTRY'S FLAG

*T*HIS is my country's flag,
  And I am my country's boy!
To love and serve her well
  Will ever be my joy.

Juniata Stafford

OLD FLAG

*W*HAT shall I say to you, Old Flag?
  You are so grand in every fold,
So linked with mighty deeds of old,
So steeped in blood where heroes fell,
So torn and pierced by shot and shell,

[178]

Old Flag

So calm, so still, so firm, so true,
My throat swells at the sight of you,
                    Old Flag.

What of the men who lifted you, Old Flag,
Upon the top of Bunker's Hill,
Who crushed the Briton's cruel will,
'Mid shock and roar and crash and scream,
Who crossed the Delaware's frozen stream,
Who starved, who fought, who bled, who died,
That you might float in glorious pride,
                    Old Flag?

What of the women brave and true, Old Flag,
Who, while the cannon thundered wild,
Sent forth a husband, lover, child,
Who labored in the field by day,
Who, all the night long, knelt to pray,
And thought that God great mercy gave,
If only freely you might wave,
                    Old Flag?

What is your mission now, Old Flag?
What but to set all people free,
To rid the world of misery,

To guard the right, avenge the wrong,
And gather in one joyful throng
Beneath your folds in close embrace
All burdened ones of every race,
                Old Flag.

Right nobly do you lead the way, Old Flag,
Your stars shine out for liberty,
Your white stripes stand for purity,
Your crimson claims that courage high
For Honor's sake to fight and die.
Lead on against the alien shore!
We'll follow you e'en to Death's door,
                Old Flag.

Hubbard Parker

OLD FLAG FOREVER

SHE'S up there,—Old Glory,—where light·
      nings are sped;
She dazzles the nations with ripples of red;
And she'll wave for us living, or droop o'er us
      dead,—
The flag of our country forever!
She's up there,—Old Glory,—how bright the
      stars stream!

And the stripes like red signals of light are
 agleam!
And we dare for her, living, or dream the last
 dream,
'Neath the flag of our country forever!
She's up there,—Old Glory,—no tyrant-dealt
 scars,
No blur on her brightness, no stain on her stars!
The brave blood of heroes hath crimsoned her
 bars.
She's the flag of our country forever!

Frank L. Stanton

A SONG FOR FLAG DAY

*O*UT on the breeze,
 O'er land and seas,
A beautiful banner is streaming.
 Shining its stars,
 Splendid its bars,
Under the sunshine 'tis gleaming.

 Over the brave
 Long may it wave,
Peace to the world ever bringing.

[181]

While to the stars,
Linked with the bars,
Hearts will forever be singing.

Lydia Avery Coonley Ward

STAND BY THE FLAG

STAND by the flag! On land and ocean
    billow
By it your fathers stood unmoved and true,
Living, defended—dying, from their pillow,
    With their last blessing, passed it on to you.

Stand by the flag, all doubt and treason scorning!
    Believe with courage firm and faith sublime,
That it will float, until the eternal morning
    Pales in its glories all the lights of Time!

John Nichols Wilder

THE STARS AND STRIPES

RALLY round the flag, boys—
    Give it to the breeze!
That's the banner that we bore
    On the land and seas.

Brave hearts are under it,
    Let the traitors brag,
Gallant lads, fire away!
    And fight for the flag.

Their flag is but a rag—
    Ours is the true one;
Up with the Stars and Stripes!
    Down with the new one!

Let our colors fly, boys—
    Guard them day and night;
For victory is liberty,
    And God will bless the right.

James T. Fields

WE'LL FLING THE STARRY BANNER OUT

*W*E'LL fling the Starry Banner out,
    That nations from afar
May read of freedom's holy light
Grafted in stripe and star.

We'll fling the Starry Banner out,
Because it tells a story,
Of days that prompted sons and sires
To deeds of love and glory.

[183]

We'll Fling the Starry Banner Out

We'll fling the Starry Banner out,
From Maine to Golden Gate;
It breathes a love for liberty,
That kings and tyrants hate.

We'll fling the Starry Banner out,
That patriot hands unfurled;
Proudly it floats o'er land and sea,
A lamp to light the world.

We'll fling the Starry Banner out,
Nor shall a star be riven
From out its field of blue so bright,
And typical of heaven.

We'll fling the Starry Banner out,
And guard with greatest care,
Its stripes and stars, and field of blue,
In peace as well as war.

We'll fling the Starry Banner out,
So that it may become
The pride of every patriot's heart,
And a joy in every home.

William F. Knott

INDEPENDENCE
DAY

AMERICA

*M*Y country, 'tis of thee,
   Sweet land of liberty,
     Of thee I sing;
Land where my fathers died,
Land of the pilgrims' pride,
From every mountain-side
     Let freedom ring.

My native country, thee,
Land of the noble free,—
     Thy name I love;
I love thy rocks and rills,
Thy woods and templed hills;
My heart with rapture thrills
     Like that above.

Let music swell the breeze,
And ring from all the trees;
     Sweet freedom's song;
Let mortal tongues awake,
Let all that breathe partake,
Let rocks their silence break,—
     The sound prolong.

Concord Hymn

Our fathers' God, to thee,
Author of liberty,
    To thee I sing;
Long may our land be bright
With freedom's holy light;
Protect us by thy might,
    Great God our King.

Samuel Francis Smith

CONCORD HYMN

BY the rude bridge that arched the flood,
  Their flag to April's breeze unfurled,
Here once the embattled farmers stood,
And fired the shot heard round the world.

The foe long since in silence slept;
Alike the conqueror silent sleeps;
And Time the ruined bridge has swept
Down the dark stream which seaward creeps.

On this green bank, by this soft stream,
We set to-day a votive stone;
That memory may their deed redeem,
When, like our sires, our sons are gone.

Creed

Spirit, that made those heroes dare
To die, and leave their children free,
Bid Time and Nature gently spare
The shaft we raise to them and thee.

Ralph Waldo Emerson

CREED

LORD, let me not in service lag,
    Let me be worthy of our flag;
Let me remember, when I'm tried,
The sons heroic who have died
In freedom's name, and in my way
Teach me to be as brave as they.

In all I am, in all I do,
Unto our flag I would be true;
For God and country let me stand.
Unstained of soul and clean of hand,
Teach me to serve and guard and love
The Starry Flag which flies above.

Edgar A. Guest

FOURTH OF JULY

*D*AY of glory: Welcome day:
  Freedom's banners greet thy ray;
See! how cheerfully they play
  With thy morning breeze,
On the rocks where pilgrims kneeled
On the heights where squadrons wheeled,
When a tyrant's thunder pealed
  O'er the trembling seas.

God of armies: did thy stars
On their courses smite his cars,
Blast his arm, and wrest his bars
  From the heaving tide?
On our standard, lo: they burn,
And when days like this return,
Sparkle o'er the soldier's urn
  Who for freedom died.

God of peace: whose spirit fills
All the echoes of our hills,
All the murmur of our rills,
  Now the storm is o'er,

[190]

Fourth of July Ode

O let freemen be our sons,
And let future Washingtons
Rise, to lead their valiant ones
    Till there's war no more!

FOURTH OF JULY ODE

OUR fathers fought for liberty;
    They struggled long and well,
History of their deeds can tell—
But did they leave us free?

Are we free from vanity,
Free from pride, and free from self,
Free from love of power and pelf,
From everything that's beggarly?

Are we free from stubborn will,
From low hate and malice small,
From opinion's tyrant thrall?
Are none of us our own slaves still?

Are we free to speak our thought,
To be happy, and be poor,
Free to enter Heaven's door,
To live and labor as we ought?
[191]

Are we, then, made free at last
From the fear of what men say,
Free to reverence To-day,
Free from slavery of the Past?

Our fathers fought for liberty;
They struggled long and well,
History of their deeds can tell—
But *ourselves* must set us free.

James Russell Lowell

NATION'S BIRTHDAY

RING out the joy bells!   Once again,
   With waving flags and rolling drums
We greet the Nation's Birthday, when,
In glorious majesty it comes.
Ah, day of days!   Alone it stands,
While, like a halo round it cast,
The radiant work of patriot hands,
Shines the bright record of the past.

Among the nations of the earth,
What land hath story like our own?
No thought of conquest marked her birth;

New National Hymn

No greed of power was ever shown
By those who crossed the ocean wild,
That they might plant upon her sod
A home for Peace and virtue mild,
And altars rear to Freedom's God.

The right that conquered, and whose power
Is shown in our broad land today;
Shown in this bright and prosperous hour
When peace and plenty gild our way;
Shown in the glorious song that swells
The hearts of men from South to North,
And in its rapturous accents tells
The story of our glorious Fourth.

Mary E. Van Dyne

NEW NATIONAL HYMN

*H*AIL, Freedom! thy bright crest
　　And gleaming shield, thrice blest
Mirror the glories of a world thine own.
Hail, heaven-born Peace!　Our sight,
Led by thy gentle light,
Shows us the paths with deathless flowers strewn,
Peace, daughter of a strife,
Abide with us till strife be lost in endless time,

New National Hymn

Honor the few who shared
Freedom's first fight, and dared
To face war's desperate tide at full flood;
Who fell on hard won ground,
And into Freedom's round
Poured the sweet balsam of their brave heart's
  blood.
They fell, but o'er that glorious grave
Floats free the banner of the cause they died to
  save.

Father, whose mighty power
Shields us through life's short hour,
To thee we pray: Bless us and keep us free;
All that is past forgive;
Teach us henceforth to live
That, through our country we may honor Thee;
And when this mortal life shall cease,
Take thou, at last, our souls to Thine eternal
  peace.

Francis Marion Crawford

THE REPUBLIC

*T*HOU, too, sail on, O Ship of State!
    Sail on, O Union, strong and great!
Humanity, with all its fears,
With all the hopes of future years,
Is hanging breathless on thy fate!
We know what Master laid thy keel,
What Workmen wrought thy ribs of steel,
Who made each mast, and sail, and rope,
What anvils rang, what hammers beat,
In what a forge and what a heat
Were forged the anchors of thy hope!
Fear not each sudden sound and shock,—
'Tis of the wave and not the rock;
'Tis but the flapping of the sail,
And not a rent made by the gale!
In spite of rock, and tempest's roar,
In spite of false lights on the shore,
Sail on, nor fear to breast the sea!
Our hearts, our hopes are all with thee,
Our hearts, our hopes, our prayers, our tears,
Our faith, triumphant o'er our fears,
Are all with thee.—are all with thee!

Henry Wadsworth Longfellow

THE STAR–SPANGLED BANNER

O SAY, can you see, by the dawn's early light,
   What so proudly we hailed at the twilight's
last gleaming?
Whose broad stripes and bright stars, through
   the perilous fight,
O'er the ramparts we watched were so gallantly
   streaming!
And the rocket's red glare, the bombs bursting
   in air,
Gave proof through the night that our flag was
   still there;
O! say, does that star-spangled banner yet wave
O'er the land of the free, and the home of the
   brave?

On that shore dimly seen through the mists of
   the deep,
Where the foe's haughty host in dread silence
   reposes,
What is that which the breeze, o'er the towering
   steep,
As it fitfully blows, now conceals, now discloses?
Now it catches the gleam of the morning's first
   beam,

In full glory reflected now shines on the stream;
'Tis the star-spangled banner; O long may it
wave
O'er the land of the free, and the home of the
brave!

And where is that band who so vauntingly swore
That the havoc of war and the battle's con-
fusion
A home and a country should leave us no more?
Their blood has washed out their foul footsteps'
pollution.
No refuge could save the hireling and slave
From the terror of flight, or the gloom of the
grave;
And the star-spangled banner in triumph doth
wave
O'er the land of the free, and the home of the
brave.

O! thus be it ever, when freemen shall stand
Between their loved homes and the war's desolation!
Blest with victory and peace, may the heav'n-
rescued land

Praise the power that hath made and preserved
  us a nation.
Then conquer we must, when our cause it is
  just,
And this be our motto—"In God is our trust:"
And the star-spangled banner in triumph shall
  wave
O'er the land of the free, and the home of the
  brave.

Francis Scott Key

LABOR
DAY

THE LAY OF THE LABORER

A SPADE! a rake! a hoe!
 A pickaxe, or a bill!
A hook to reap, or a scythe to mow,
 A flail, or what ye will,
And here's a ready hand
 To ply the needful tool,
And skilled enough, by lessons rough,
 In Labor's rugged school.

To hedge, or dig the ditch,
 To lop or fell the tree,
To lay the swathe on the sultry field,
 Or plough the stubborn lea;
The harvest stack to bind,
 The wheaten rick to thatch,
And never fear in my pouch to find
 The tinder or the match.

*   *   *   *   *   *   *

No parish money, or loaf,
 No pauper badges for me,

The Lay of The Laborer

A son of the soil, by right of toil
    Entitled to my fee.
No alms I ask, give me my task;
    Here are the arm, the leg,
The strength, the sinews of a Man,
    To work, and not to beg.

Still one of Adam's heirs,
    Though doomed by chance of birth
To dress so mean, and to eat the lean
    Instead of the fat of the earth;
To make such humble meals
    As honest labor can,
A bone and a crust, with a grace to God,
    And little thanks to man!

A spade! a rake! a hoe!
    A pickaxe, or a bill!
A hook to reap, or a scythe to mow,
    A flail, or what ye will;
Whatever the tool to ply,
    Here is a willing drudge,
With muscle and limb, and woe to him
    Who does their pay begrudge!

Thomas Hood

NIGHT COMETH

*W*ORK, for the night is coming,
   Work through the morning hours;
Work while the dew is sparkling,
   Work 'mid springing flowers;
Work when the day grows brighter,
   Work in the glowing sun;
Work, for the night is coming,
   When man's work is done.

Work, for the night is coming,
   Work through the sunny noon;
Fill brightest hours with labor,
   Rest comes sure and soon:
Give every flying minute
   Something to keep in store;
Work, for the night is coming
   When man works no more.

Work, for the night is coming,
   Under the sunset skies;
While their bright tints are glowing,
   Work, for daylight flies:
Work, till the last beam fadeth,

Fadeth to shine no more;
Work, while the night is darkening,
When man's work is o'er.

Sidney Dyer

A SONG OF WORK

*W*ORK while the sun climbeth high in the
    heaven,
Work in the noon-day's dust and heat,
Work till the evening its blessing hath given,
Work while the moon keeps vigil sweet.
Work while the verdant grasses are springing,
Work in the summer's radiant glow,
Work in the autumn with gladness and singing,
Work in the time of frost and snow.

Labor is noble and rich is its guerdon,
Sweet after toil comes peaceful rest.
Take on thy shoulders, rejoicing, the burden,
Pleasure is good, but work is best.
Great is our Lord, of labor the master;
Follow the path His feet have trod.
Strive, with the joy of all honest endeavor;
Then at the last, find rest with God.

Mary Blake

WORK

WORK!
  Thank God for the might of it,
The ardor, the urge, the delight of it,
Work that springs from the heart's desire,
Setting the brain and the soul on fire—
Oh, what is so good as the heat of it,
And what is so glad as the beat of it,
And what is so kind as the stern command,
Challenging brain and heart and hand?

Work!
Thank God for the pride of it,
For the beautiful, conquering tide of it,
Sweeping the life in its furious flood,
Thrilling the arteries, cleansing the blood,
Mastering stupor and dull despair,
Moving the dreamer to do and dare.
Oh, what is so good as the urge of it,
And what is so glad as the surge of it,
And what is so strong as the summons deep,
Rousing the torpid soul from sleep?

Work!
Thank God for the pace of it,
For the terrible, keen, swift race of it;

Work

Fiery steeds in full control,
Nostrils a-quiver to greet the goal.
Work, the Power that drives behind,
Guiding the purposes, taming the mind,
Holding the runaway wishes back,
Reining the will to one steady track,
Speeding the energies faster, faster,
Triumphing over disaster.
Oh, what is so good as the pain of it,
And what is so kind as the cruel goad,
Forcing us on through the rugged road?

Work!
Thank God for the swing of it,
For the clamoring, hammering ring of it,
Passion and labor daily hurled
On the mighty anvils of the world,
Oh, what is so fierce as the flame of it?
And what is so huge as the aim of it?
Thundering on through dearth and doubt,
Calling the plan of the Maker out.
Work, the Titan: Work, the friend,
Shaping the earth to a glorious end,
Draining the swamps and blasting the hills,
Doing whatever the Spirit wills—
Rending a continent apart,

Work

To answer the dream of the Master heart,
Thank God for a world where none may shirk—
Thank God for the splendor of work!

Angela Morgan

WORK

*L*ET me but do my work from day to day,
    In field or forest, at the desk or loom,
  In roaring market-place or tranquil room;
Let me but find it in my heart to say,
When vagrant wishes beckon me astray,
  "This is my work; my blessing, not my doom;
  "Of all who live, I am the one by whom
"This work can best be done in the right way."

Then shall I see it not too great, nor small,
    To suit my spirit and to prove my powers;
    Then shall I cheerfully greet the laboring
      hours,
And cheerfully turn, when the long shadows fall
    At eventide, to play and love and rest,
    Because I know for me my work is best.

Henry van Dyke

COLUMBUS
DAY

THE BOY COLUMBUS

'TIS a wonderful story," I hear you say,
    "How he struggled and worked and plead
    and prayed,
And faced every danger undismayed,
With a will that would neither break nor bend.
And discovered a new world in the end—
But what does it teach to a boy of today?
All the worlds are discovered, you know of
    course,
All the rivers are traced to their utmost source:
If he had ever so much a mind
    To become a discoverer famous;
And if we'd much rather read a book
About someone else, and the risks he took,
    Why nobody, surely, can blame us."

So you think all the worlds are discovered now;
All the lands have been charted and sailed about,
Their mountains climbed, their secrets found out;
All the seas have been sailed, and their currents
    known—

To the uttermost isles the winds have blown
They have carried a venturing prow?
Yet there lie all about us new worlds, every-
 where,
That wait their discoverer's footfall; spread fair
Are electrical worlds that no eye has yet seen,
And mechanical worlds that lie hidden serene
 And await their Columbus securely.
There are new worlds in Science and new worlds
 in Art.
And the boy who will work with his head and his
 heart
 Will discover his new world surely.

         Anonymous

CHRISTOPHER COLUMBUS

CHRISTOPHER COLUMBUS, where would
 I be
If you had never crossed the sea,
If you had never thought the earth a ball,
If you had never cared to sail at all?
Suppose the kind Queen Isabel
Had loved her jewels far too well
To sell them for a sailor true

Christopher Columbus

Like you,
Christopher Columbus;
Suppose your small ships made of wood,
Were not so trusty, strong, and good,
We should not keep your day each year,
And I should not be standing here;
Perhaps I'd live far, far away
And never know Columbus Day.
My house and every building tall—
The school would not be here at all;
Along the street where people go
Only strong, strong trees would grow;
And everywhere on lake and hill
The land would be quite dark and still,
With only wigwams on the ground
And Indian children walking round,
And not a stars and stripes in sight
At evening or in morning light!

O dear, I wonder where I'd be
If you had never crossed the sea,
Christopher Columbus;
I like it better far this way;
I like to live at home and play;
And so I'll keep Columbus Day!

[213]

Columbus

I'm glad you sailed, I'm glad you knew
The earth is round; I'm glad the good queen
    trusted you,
I'm glad you were so brave and wise and true!
Christopher Columbus.

Annette Wynne

COLUMBUS

*T*HE night air brings strange whisperings—
    vague scents—
Over the unknown ocean, which his dreams
Had spanned with visions of new continents;
Fragrance of clove and cedar, and the balms
With which the heavy tropic forest teems
With murmur as of wind among the palms.

They breathe across the high deck where he
    stands
With far set eyes, as one who dreams awake
Waiting sure dawn of undiscovered lands;
Till on the slow lift of the purple swells,
The golden radiances of morning break
Lighting the emblazoned sails of Caravels.

[214]

By inadvertence, these four stanzas of Mr. Going's poem in STAR-
GLOW AND SONG, Harper, 1909, were presented in former editions
as an entire composition. They are only the first movement.

Then from the foremost sounds a sudden cry—
The old world's startled greeting to the new—
For lo! the land, across the western sky!
The exultant land: Oh long-starved hopes,
    black fears,
Gibings of courtiers, mutinies of crew—
Answered forever, as that shore appears.

Great Master Dreamer! Grander than Cathay,
Richer than India—this new Western World
Shall flourish when Castile has passed away.
Not even thy gigantic vision spanned
Its future, as with cross and flag unfurled,
Thy deep Te Deum sounded on the strand.

Charles Buxton Going

COLUMBUS

*G*IVE me white paper!
    This which you use is black and rough
      with smears
Of sweat and grime, and fraud, and blood and
      tears,
Crossed with the story of men's sins and fears,
Of battle and of famine all these years,

[215]

When all God's children had forgot their
   birth
And drudged and fought and died like beasts
   of earth.

   "Give me white paper!"
One storm-trained seaman listened to the word;
What no man saw he saw, he heard what no man
   heard.
   In answer he compelled the sea
   To eager man to tell
   The secret she had kept so well!
Left blood and guilt and tyranny behind—
Sailing still west the hidden shore to find;
   For all mankind that unstained scroll un-
      furled,
   Where God might write anew the story of the
      World.

Edward Everett Hale

COLUMBUS

(January, 1487)

ST. STEPHEN'S cloistered hall was proud
   In learning's pomp that day,
For there a robed and stately crowd

Pressed on in long array.
A mariner with simple chart
   Confronts that conclave high,
While strong ambition stirs his heart,
And burning thoughts of wonder dart
   From lip and sparkling eye.

What hath he said? With frowning face,
   In whispered tones they speak,
And lines upon their tablets trace,
   Which flush each ashen cheek;
The Inquisition's mystic doom
   Sits on their brows severe,
And bursting forth in visioned gloom,
Sad heresy from burning tomb
   Groans on the startled ear.

Courage, thou Genoese! Old Time
   Thy splendid dream shall crown;
Yon Western Hemisphere sublime,
   Where unshorn forests frown,
The awful Andes' cloud-wrapped brow,
   The Indian hunter's bow,
Bold streams untamed by helm or prow,
And rocks of gold and diamonds, thou
   To thankless Spain shall show.

Columbus

Courage, World-finder! Thou hast need!
   In Fate's unfolding scroll,
Dark woes and ingrate wrongs I read,
   That rack the noble soul.
On! on! Creation's secrets probe,
   Then drink thy cup of scorn,
And wrapped in fallen Cæsar's robe,
Sleep like that master of the globe,
   All glorious,—yet forlorn.

Lydia Huntley Sigourney

COLUMBUS

*A*N Italian boy that liked to play
   In Genoa about the ships all day,
With curly head and dark, dark eyes,
That gazed at earth in child surprise;
And dreamed of distant stranger skies.

He watched the ships that came crowding in
With cargo of riches; he loved the din
Of the glad rush out and the spreading sails
And the echo of far-off windy gales.

He studied the books of the olden day;
He studied but knew far more than they;

Columbus Day

He talked to the learned men of the school—
So wise he was they thought him a fool,
A fool with the dark, dark, dreamful eyes,
A child he was—grown wonder-wise.

Youth and dreams are over, past
And out, far out he is sailing fast
Toward the seas he dreamed;—strange lands
   arise—
The world is made rich by his great emprise—
And the wisest know he was more than wise.

Annette Wynne

COLUMBUS DAY

*D*O you wonder to see him in chains
   Whom once the King rose from his throne
  to greet?
At Barcelona—the city decked herself
To meet me, roared my name; the King and
  Queen
Bade me be seated, speak, and tell them all
The story of my voyage, and while I spoke
The crowd's roar fell,
And when I ceased to speak, the King and
  Queen

Sank from their thrones, and melted into tears,
And knelt, and lifted hand and voice
In praise to God who led me thro' the waste.

And now you see me in chains!
Chains for him who gave a new heaven, a new
  earth,
Gave glory and more empire to the Kings
Of Spain than did all their battles! Chains for
  him
Who pushed his prows into the setting sun,
And made West East, and sail'd into the
  Dragon's mouth,
And came upon the Mountain of the World,
And saw the rivers fall from Paradise!

Eighteen long years of waste, seven in your
  Spain,
Lost, showing courts and King a truth,—the
  earth a sphere.
At Salamanca we fronted the learning of all
  Spain,
All their cosmogonies, their astronomies;
No guesswork! I was certain of my goal;
At last their Highnesses were half-assured this
  earth might be a sphere.

Palos, Spain, 1492

Last night a dream I had—I sail'd
On my first voyage, harass'd by the frights
Of my first crew, their curses and their groans.
The compass, like an old friend false at last
In our most need, appall'd them, and the wind
Still westward, and the weedy seas—at length
The landbird, and the branch with berries on it,
The carven staff—and at last the light, the light
   on Salvador.

All glory to God!
I have accomplished what I came to do.
I pray you tell King Ferdinand
That I am loyal to him even unto death.

Alfred Lord Tennyson

PALOS, SPAIN, 1492

*W*HAT a stir in the harbor!
   What a stir in the street!
What a stowing of cargo
   And noisy hurrying feet!

What a stir on the quay steps
   As the boats turn out to sea;

Palos, Spain, 1492

Were ever ships half so gallant
   As Columbus' little three?

What a waving of kerchiefs;
   What a stir in the breast;
What a tumult of feeling
   As the ships dropped into the West.

    *   *   *   *   *   *   *

What a stir in Palos
   When the *Niña* came again;
What a ringing of mad wild bells
   What a fêting of men!

What a stir in the earth and air
   As the mighty truth unfurled,
Three ships and a crew and a great, great soul—
   Columbus—had found a world!

Annette Wynne

ROOSEVELT'S BIRTHDAY

BOY OF OLD MANHATTAN

A BOY of old Manhattan,
A boy as you and I,
Once watched its towers rising
Until they spanned the sky.

A boy of old Manhattan,
With granite in his soul,
Beheld the star of Lincoln
Above his steepled goal!

A boy of old Manhattan
Built upward hour by hour;
The edifice he visioned
Became a nation's tower!

Morris Abel Beer

IN THE COVE

T HERE'S a hill above the harbor
Which ebbs and flows beneath it there—
A small hill, a grassy hill,
The path is rough and steep;

In the Cove

The pine-trees sing above it,
And creeping vines enwreath it there—
The little quiet hilltop
Where the Colonel lies asleep.

The circling seagulls wheel above
When winter gales blow over it;
The song-birds build their nests there,
And rabbits run and play;
The locust-trees drop scented flowers,
And moss and myrtle cover it,
And the wind brings whiffs of sea-salt
From the white-caps on the bay.

Close, close within the heart of home
The soldier lays him down at last;
Deep in the quiet Cove he loved
The hunter is at rest;
The Heart of all the Nation sleeps
Upon our tiny hill at last,
While all the trumpets sound for him
Beyond the shining West.

Mary Fanny Youngs

OUR COLONEL

*D*EEP loving, well knowing
   His world and its blindness,
A heart overflowing
With measureless kindness,

Undaunted in labor
(And Death was a trifle),
Steel true as a sabre,
Direct as a rifle.

All Man in his doing,
All Boy in his laughter,
He fronted, unerring,
The Now and Hereafter.

A storm-battling cedar,
A comrade, a brother—
Oh, such was our Leader,
Beloved as no other!

When weaker souls faltered
His courage remade us
Whose tongue never paltered,
Who never betrayed us.

His hand on your shoulder
All honors exceeding,
What breast but was bolder,
Because he was leading!

And still in our trouble,
In peace or in war-time,
His word shall redouble
Our strength as afore-time.

When wrongs cry for righting,
No odds shall appall us;
To clean honest fighting
Again he will call us,

And, cow-boys, or dough-boys,
We'll follow his drum, boys,
Who never said, "Go, boys!"
But always said, "Come, boys!"

Arthur Guiterman

THE PROPHET

A MERICA has nourished wiser sons,
    More cultured men have graced her halls
  of state
But Roosevelt she destined to be great,
And he is now among her deathless ones.

[228]

Roosevelt

Smooth words he scorned, hypocrisy he
    spurned;
The truth to him was as a fiery sword;
He stood a mighty prophet of the Lord
To scourge the wrong, though flames about him
    burned,
His judgment erred, his conscience never failed;
Through fateful nights, within his dauntless
    heart
The great light gleamed which was of him a part;
His courage waxed when lesser spirits quailed.
Through all the years shall live this sovereign
    man.
Stout heart, high mind, great-souled American.

Thomas Curtis Clark

ROOSEVELT

*H*E came out the void
    Buoyed upon the surging tides.
He braved the West,
Defied the wide frontiers;
He trekked the continents
And enthroned his name
Among the white, the black, the brown, the
    yellow men.

Theodore Roosevelt

He trod the frond,
Fording the darkened streams
That glide through jungles
To the tropic sea.
He spanned the globe,
He swept the skies,
And moved beneath the eaters of the deep.
He entered all the portals of the world.
A vibrant, thrilled, exhaustless, restless soul;
Riding at last the very stars—
Asleep.

Robert H. Davis

THEODORE ROOSEVELT

*H*IS name, when uttered, thrills the world
   And charms its millions through
And flags of nations are unfurled
   In honor of his name so great and true.

   *   *   *   *   *   *

A life of vigor he had wrought;
   He labored to the end;
A man of vision and forethought—
   The common people's friend.

   *   *   *   *   *   *

Theodore Roosevelt

He loved and served his country's laws
   With devotion deep and true.
This heart was wrapped in Freedom's cause,
   His life inspires us thru and thru.

    *   *   *   *   *   *

The spirit of true Americanism
   He preached and practiced, too:
His great heart burned with patriotism
   That thrilled the nation through.

    *   *   *   *   *   *

He blessed the world in many ways;
   His vision reached afar;
Like the sun sends forth its rays,
   His life's a blazing star.

    *   *   *   *   *   *

High in the hall of matchless fame
   Where the names of heroes blaze,
We'll write his wondrous glorious name
   As the world joins in his praise.

William W. Peavyhouse

VALIANT FOR TRUTH

VALIANT for Truth has gone—Alas, that he
    has left us,
  Valiant for Truth, the leader that we love
Where shall we find his like? Grim death, thou
    hast bereft us
  Of that great force that lifted us above.

Valiant for Truth, thy voice rang strong, and
    clear, and loudly,
  We had not borne to have its accents fail;
Nor would we choose, O Knight, that thou
    shouldst go less proudly
  Ardent and young, upon the last, long trail.

What though we stumble blindly over ways that
    darken,
  We are not worthy if we do not fare
Forth to the West, where still thy voice calls
    us to hearken—
    Up to the heights, and we shall meet thee
    there.

Who Goes There?

"Valiant for Truth has come," thus all the
    trumpets sounded,
Valiant for Truth who faltered not, nor fell;
Fearless he rode the trail, the last long trail
    unbounded,
    Rode to the final goal, where·all is well.

Corinne Roosevelt Robinson

WHO GOES THERE?

WHO goes there?   An American!
    Brain and spirit, brawn and heart.
Twas for him that the nations spared
Each to the years its noblest part,
Till from the Dutch, the Gaul, and Celt
Blossomed the soul of Roosevelt.

Student, trooper, and gentleman,
Level lidded with times and kings,
His the voice for the comrades' cheer;
His the ear when the sabre rings.
Then shades of the old days melt
In the quick glance of Roosevelt.

Who Goes There?

Hand that's moulded to hilt of sword,
Heart that ever has laughed at fear,
Type and pattern of civic pride,
Wit and grace of the cavalier.
All that his fathers prayed and felt
Gleams in the glance of Roosevelt.

Who goes there?   An American!
Man to the core as men should be.
Let him pass through the line alone,
Type of the sons of liberty.
Here where his fathers' fathers dwelt
Honor and faith for Roosevelt.

Grace Duffie Boylan

ARMISTICE
DAY

AMERICA'S ANSWER

R EST ye in peace, ye Flanders dead,
⠀⠀The fight that ye so bravely led
We've taken up. And we will keep
True faith with you who lie asleep
With each a cross to mark his bed,
And poppies blowing overhead,
Where once his own life blood ran red.
So let your rest be sweet and deep
⠀⠀⠀⠀In Flanders fields.

Fear not that ye have died for naught,
The torch ye threw to us we caught.
Ten million hands will hold it high,
And Freedom's light shall never die!
We've learned the lesson that ye taught
⠀⠀⠀⠀In Flanders fields.

⠀⠀⠀⠀⠀⠀⠀⠀⠀⠀⠀⠀⠀⠀*R. W. Lillard*

ARMISTICE NIGHT

L EST we forget!
⠀⠀The months swing into years,
Our souls are caught in trivial things again.

For Remembrance

We laugh at what we once beheld with tears.
In petty strife we ease our souls their pain.
Lest we forget!

Curtis Wheeler

FOR REMEMBRANCE

*W*HAT is it, O dear Country of our pride,
  We pledge anew that we will not forget?
To keep on Freedom's altar burning yet
The fires for which a myriad heroes died
Known and unknown, beyond the far sea's tide
That their great gift be no futility.

Faith with the Dead kept through our living
    faith;
  In this alone the true remembrance lies,
  The unfading garland for the sacrifice,
To prove their dream of Brotherhood no wraith,
No moment's hope—its birth-pang one with
    death—
But the fixed goal of our humanity.

Basil Ebers

FORGET-ME-NOT DAY

$\mathcal{S}$HALL we forget, when Nations meet,
To join again the broken ties—
The days of War, and marching feet
Beneath the stars of other skies—
Or will the years
Have dimmed the tears
And longing in our eyes?

Shall we forget the crowded graves,
Blood-stained beneath a wooden cross,
And bodies in the restless waves
That undiscovered float and toss,—
Or will our pride in those who died
Repay us for our loss?

Shall we forget the ones so brave—
The aviators of the sky,
When comrades, on a hurried grave,
Dropped tribute flowers from on high?
So much to give,
So good to live,
And yet they had to die.

In Flanders Fields

Shall we forget the shattered nerves,
   Disabled forms and twisted minds,
And those for whom the Darkness serves
   Because the war has left them blind?
Oh! it is they
Who still must pay,
   And need a world that's kind.

Nan Terrell Reed

IN FLANDERS FIELDS

*I*N Flanders fields the poppies blow
   Between the crosses, row on row,
That mark our place; and in the sky
The larks, still bravely singing, fly
Scarce heard amid the guns below.

We are the dead: Short days ago
We lived, felt dawn, saw sunset glow,
Loved and were loved, and now we lie
In Flanders fields.

Take up our quarrel with the foe!
To you from failing hands we throw
The Torch. Be yours to hold it high!

In Flanders Fields

If ye break faith with us who die
We shall not sleep, though poppies grow,
In Flanders fields.

John D. McCrae

IN FLANDERS FIELDS

(An Answer)

IN Flanders fields the cannon boom
And fitful flashes light the gloom,
While up above, like eagles, fly
The fierce destroyers of the sky;
With stains the earth wherein you lie
Is redder than the poppy bloom,
In Flanders fields.

Sleep on, ye brave. The shrieking shell,
The quaking trench, the startled yell,
The fury of the battle hell
Shall wake you not, for all is well.
Sleep peacefully for all is well.

Your flaming torch aloft we bear,
With burning heart on oath we swear

[241]

To keep the faith, to fight it through,
To crush the foe or sleep with you
    In Flanders fields.

C. B. Galbreath

MEMORIAL DAY

I HEARD a cry in the night from a far-flung
    host,
From a host that sleeps through the years the
    last long sleep,
By the Meuse, by the Marne, in the Argonne's
    shattered wood,
In a thousand rose-thronged churchyards
    through our land.
Sleeps! Do they sleep? I know I heard their
    cry,
Shrilling along the night like a trumpet blast:

"We died," they cried, "for a dream. Have
    ye forgot?
We dreamed of a world reborn whence wars
    had fled,
Where swords were broken in pieces and guns
    were rust,

Where the poor man dwelt in quiet, the rich
  in peace,
And children played in the streets, joyous and
  free.
We thought we could sleep content in the task
  well done;
But the rumble of guns rolls over us, iron upon
  iron
Sounds from the forge where are fashioned
  guns anew;
New fleets spring up in new seas, and under
  the wave
Stealthy new terrors swarm, with embowelled
  death.
Fresh cries of hate ring out loud from the demagogue's throat,
While greed reaches out afresh to grasp new
  lands.
Have we died in vain, in vain? Is our dream
  denied?
You men who live on the earth we bought with
  our woe,
Will ye stand idly by while they shape new
  wars,

Or will ye rise, who are strong, to fulfill our
   dream,
To silence the demagogue's voice, to crush the
   fools
Who play with the blood-stained toys that
   crowd new graves?
We call, we call in the night, will ye hear and
   heed?"

In the name of our dead will we hear?   Will
   we grant them sleep?

William E. Brooks

OUR DEAD HEROES

*R*EST on, O heroes! in your silent slumber!
   Hail and farewell, ye mighty, moveless
   dead!
Long as her centuries Earth shall know and
   number,
Green be the laurel boughs above ye spread.

Your course is sped; your record man remembers,
And God's own hand your sacred dust shall
   keep:

Old Soldier Dead

Though all the flame hath left those mortal
    embers,
Upward it sprang, with bright, immortal leap.

Sleep in your country's heart; forever holy
Your memory shines along the slopes we tread;
Another hundred years their incense lowly
Ere long shall o'er your sculptured honors shed.

And we who bring you grace and salutation,
We, too, shall sleep; and nobler tribes of men
Shall offer here the homage of a nation
Rich with a wisdom far beyond our ken.

But still, as years return, shall man returning
Fight, fall, despair, or chant the conqueror's
    psalm,
Still the same light in patriot hearts be burning,
And Heaven, still just, bestow the martyr's palm.

Rose Terry Cooke

OLD SOLDIER DEAD

*I*N Flanders fields, where poppies blow,
    In France where beauteous roses glow,
There let them rest—forever sleep,
While we eternal vigil keep

Old Soldier Dead

With our heart's love—with our soul's pray'r,
For all our Fallen "Over There."

The sounding sea between us rolls
And in perpetual requiem tolls—
Three thousand miles of cheerless space
Lie 'twixt us and their resting place;
'Twas God who took them by the hand
And left them in the stranger land.

The earth is sacred where they fell—
Forever on it lies the spell
Of hero deeds in Freedom's cause,
And men unborn shall come and pause
To say a prayer, or bow the head;
So leave these graves to hold their dead.

Let not our sighing nor our tears
Fall on them through the coming years
Who on the land, on sea, in air,
With dauntless courage everywhere,
Their homes and country glorified—
Stood to their arms and smiling died.

Great France will leave no need nor room
That we place flowers on their tomb—

Peace

And proudly o'er their resting place,
Will float forever in its grace,
O'er cross, and star, and symbol tag,
Their own beloved country's flag.

Annette Kohn

PEACE

*P*EACE, battle-worn and starved, and gaunt
  and pale
Rises like mist upon a storm-swept shore.
Rises from out the blood-stained fields and bows
  her head,
Blessing the passionate dead
Who gladly died that she might live forevermore.

Unheeding generations come and go,
And careless men and women will forget,
Caught in the whirling loom. Who tapestried
  To-day
Flings Yesterday away,
And covers up the crimsoned West whose sun
  has set.

But faithful ghosts, like shepherds, will return
To call the flocking shades and break with them

Love-bread, and Peace will strain them to her
    breast, and weep,
And deathless vigil keep.
Yea, Peace, while worlds endure, will sing their
    requiem.

G. O. Warren

REMEMBERING DAY

*A*LL the soldiers marching along;
        All the children singing a song;
All the flowers dewy and sweet;
All the flags hung out in the street;
Hearts that throb in a grateful way—
For this is our Remembering Day.

Mary Wight Saunders

SAINTE JEANNE

T'HERE is a little church in France to-day
    Where once a simple maiden knelt, who
now
Wears God's insignia upon her brow—
First of all the saints to whom her people pray.

[248]

Sainte Jeanne

Maid of the Lilies, warrior of the Sword,
           Jeanne d'Arc,
True soldier in the service of the Lord,
           Shall you not hark?

To-day the candles burn before your shrine,
Your banner glows within the sacred space,
But not alone, for with it, by God's grace,
There does another of its color shine;
Two and yet one—a holy thing enshrined,
           Sainte Jeanne,
Two banners at Domremy are entwined,
           Bless them as one.

There is a little church in France to-day;
How many prayers have risen thence to you!
For their sake heed another prayer and new,
Strange words yet beautiful your people say.
Bend down between the lilies and the lance,
           Sainte Jeanne.
"For those Americans who died for France,"
           Light their souls on!

There is a little church in France to-day;
Your people kneel about the altar there.
You who were warrior and woman, hear

With hands of very love this prayer they pray:
A simple prayer for those souls chivalrous
      Who dared the dark,
"For those Americans who died for us,"
      Jeanne d'Arc.

Theodosia Garrison

THE SOLDIER'S DIRGE

DEAD in the battle—dead on the field:
    More than his life can a soldier yield?
Dead for his country, muffle the drums:
Slowly the sad procession comes.
The heart may ache, but the heart must swell
With pride for the soldier who fought so well.
His blood has burnished his sabre bright;
To his memory, honor; to him, good-night.

Elizabeth Harman

TAPS

SLEEP,
    Now that the charge is won,
Sleep in the narrow clod;
Now it is set of sun,
Sleep till the trump of God.
Sleep.

To Men Unborn

Sleep.
Fame is a bugle call
Blown past a crumbling wall;
Battles are clean forgot;
Captains and towns are not;
Sleep shall outlast them all.
Sleep.

Lizette Woodworth Reese

TO MEN UNBORN

*W*HEN spring comes on with freshness of
    new leaves,
And gypsy meadows don their festive gear
Of colored blooms, and when the ploughman
    cleaves
    The rich brown earth, and skies are blue and
    clear,
When all the earth in sun goes revelling
    Until with life the autumn overflows
And new ripe fruits and grains go gathering
    To trade in towns where peaceful commerce
    flows,
Know then, O men unborn, in vain we cried
    For peace and drew forgotten swords and
    sent

The "Unknown" Dead

Our youth to battle youth—so young they died
  All careless of the precious gift they spent!
O priceless peace!   Paid for with such dear life!
  Peace seen afar through grief and hate and
    strife!

David Osborne Hamilton

THE "UNKNOWN" DEAD

*T*HE "unknown" dead?   Not so: we know
    him well,
  Who died for us on that red soil of France,
Who faced the fearful shock of gas and shell,
  And laughed at death in some blood-strewn
    advance.

Nameless, in truth, but crowned with such a
    name
  As glory gives to those who greatly die;
Who marched a single soldier, with the flame
  Of duty bidding him to Calvary.

He is all brothers dead, all lovers lost,
  All sons and comrades, resting there;
They symbol of the knightly, fallen host,
  The sacred pledge of burdens yet to bear.

The "Unknown" Dead

Mangled and torn for whom we pray today,
　Whose soul rose grandly to God's peaceful
　　throne,
Leaving to us this quiet, shattered clay,
　Silent and still—unnamed—but not un-
　known.

John R. Rathom

BOOK
WEEK

A BOOK

*T*HERE is no frigate like a book
    To take us lands away,
Nor any courser like a page
    Of prancing poetry.
This traverse may the poorest take
    Without oppress of toll;
How frugal is the chariot
    That bears a human soul!

Emily Dickinson

A BOOK

I'M a strange contradiction; I'm new, and I'm
    old,
I'm often in tatters, and oft decked with gold,
Though I never could read, yet lettered I'm
    found;
Though blind, I enlighten; though loose, I am
    bound,
I'm always in black, and I'm always in white
I'm grave and I'm gay, I am heavy and light—

Book, Book

In form too I differ,—I'm thick and I'm thin
I've no flesh and no bones, yet I'm covered with
    skin;
I've more points than the compass, more stops
    than the flute;
I sing without voice, without speaking confute.
I'm English, I'm German, I'm French, and I'm
    Dutch.
Some love me too fondly, some slight me too
    much;
I often die soon, though I sometimes live ages,
And no monarch alive has so many pages.

Hannah More

BOOK, BOOK

*B*OOK, book, I have found
    Earth, sea, air within you bound;
I have talked with saints and sages,
In your clear cool shining pages;
I have searched the skies with you,
Traced the planets through and through;
You have been my comrade brave
Or my willing, waiting slave.

A Book is an Enchanted Gate

Book, book, I have found
Earth, sea, air, within you bound;
Through your clear cool shining pages
I have walked with saints and sages.

Annette Wynne

A BOOK IS AN ENCHANTED GATE

A BOOK is an enchanted gate,
    That leads to magic lands,
But cross the threshold and your fate
    A poet's pen commands.

For on strange journeys you are led,
    Beyond your lamp-lit walls,
Where Fancy ever strides ahead
    And onward subtly calls,

Until you leave the streets behind,
    Lost in a forest maze,
And wander where the dim trails wind
    In singing, fragrant ways.

Or set adrift on castled streams,
    Where mellow moonbeams dance,

Books

You sail, a voyager of dreams,
  To regions of Romance.

So when I weary of the town,
  Its whirling dust and din,
I seek my books that never frown,
  When solace I would win.

For they, good friends in tale and rhyme,
  Have never failed to bring
In troubled hours of autumn time,
  The lilac days of spring!

Morris Abel Beer

BOOKS

BOOKS, books that I love so,
  Poetry . . . fairy-tales . . . stories . . .
All of them together make one huge book
Broad as a mountain
With golden pages
And pictures of long ago.
I read and I read . . . of living . . . of
  thoughts . . .
Of queer things people tell:

Books

If I could I would buy that huge book,
All the world in one!
But it cannot be bought
For one penny or two.

Hilda Conkling

BOOKS

*M*Y neighbor's books sit primly in a row—
    Dickens in blue, and Thackeray in red,
Like Orphans dressed in their asylum gowns,
With only numbers to distinguish them:
And, like the Orphans, they are coldly clean;
No dog's-eared pages there—no pencil marks;
Even the dust is kept from them by glass;
And there they sit, encloistered and aloof.

My books are not like that; they are my friends;
They share my sorrow and they share my joy—
Live as I live, and show their age, like me;
Here's one has covers faded from the sun—
It shared my holiday along the shore;
This one companions me at breakfast-time,
Each morning as I take my hasty meal,
And gives me courage for the day's despite.
(It's rather spotty, true; but, ah, so dear!)

And each one has its own distinctive dress;
A set of poets? Never!
      Keats and Poe—
Imagine them attired in uniform!
My Keats wears purple, and my Poe wears gray;
And both are marked with many pencilings,
And open at my favorite passages
With sweet garrulity.
      You lonely books
Upon my neighbor's shelves, I pity you!

         Florence Van Cleve

BOOKS ARE KEYS

*B*OOKS are keys to wisdom's treasure;
 Books are gates to lands of pleasure;
Books are paths that upward lead;
Books are friends. Come let us read.

         Emilie Poulsson

BOOKS ARE SOLDIERS

*B*OOKS are soldiers gaily dressed, standing
 grave and tall,
Like a halting regiment close against the wall;
They have marched through many lands, over
 meadows green,

[262]

Cities great and monuments and rivers they have
    seen;
All year long they wait to tell you wondrous
    things they know
If you'll only listen;—Soldiers in a row,
Tell me what you have to tell,
Of the things you know so well;
Tell me, soldiers, gaily dressed, standing grave
    and tall,
Like a halting regiment, close against the wall.

Annette Wynne

MY BOOK HOLDS MANY STORIES

*M*Y book holds many stories, wrapped
    tightly in itself,
And yet it never makes a noise but waits upon
    my shelf
Until I come and take it; then soon my book
    and I
Are sailing on a fairy sea or floating in the sky.

Annette Wynne

THE NICEST STORY

I'M going to write a story,
  The bestest ever told—
The kind that little chil'ren like,
  Jus' my years old.

There's crockendiles 'n' fairies,
  'N' chil'ren in a shoe,
'N' animals who talk aloud,
  'N' a Princess, too!

There's dragons on the first page,
  'N' giants all the way;
'N' it's going on forever,
  Forever and a day.

The nicest tales do finish,
  'N' that is always sad.
But this will have no ending,—
  Oh, aren't you very glad?

I'll write, and write, and write it,
  'N' then you'll read and read.
Oh, THAT's the nicest story,
  The kind that chil'ren need.

Abbie Farwell Brown

READING

    . . . We get no good
By being ungenerous even to a book,
   And calculating profits . . . so much help
By so much reading. It is rather when
We gloriously forget ourselves and plunge
Soul-forward, headlong, into a book's profound,
Impassioned for its beauty and salt of truth—
'Tis then we get the right good from a book.

Elizabeth Browning

WHEN MOTHER READS ALOUD

*W*HEN Mother reads aloud, the past
    Seems real as every day;
I hear the tramp of armies vast,
I see the spears and lances cast,
   I join the thrilling fray;
Brave knights and ladies fair and proud
I meet when Mother reads aloud.

When Mother reads aloud, far lands
   Seem very near and true;
I cross the deserts' gleaming sands,
[265]

Or hunt the jungle's prowling bands,
   Or sail the ocean blue.
Far heights, whose peaks the cold mists shroud,
I scale, when Mother reads aloud.

When Mother reads aloud, I long
   For noble deeds to do—
To help the right, redress the wrong;
It seems so easy to be strong,
   So simple to be true.
Oh, thick and fast the visions crowd
My eyes, when Mother reads aloud.

Unknown

THANKSGIVING
DAY

LANDING OF THE PILGRIM FATHERS

*T*HE breaking waves dashed high
   On the stern and rock-bound coast,
And the woods, against a stormy sky,
   Their giant branches tossed;

And the heavy night hung dark
   The hills and waters o'er,
When a band of exiles moored their bark
   On the wild New England shore.

Not as the conqueror comes,
   They, the true-hearted, came:
Not with the roll of the stirring drums,
   And the trumpet that sings of fame;

Not as the flying come,
   In silence and in fear,—
They shook the depths of the desert's gloom
   With their hymns of lofty cheer.

[269]

Amidst the storm they sang,
  And the stars heard, and the sea;
And the sounding aisles of the dim woods rang
  To the anthem of the free!

The ocean-eagle soared
  From his nest by the white wave's foam,
And the rocking pines of the forest roared:
  This was their welcome home!

There were men with hoary hair
  Amidst that pilgrim band;
Why have they come to wither there,
  Away from their childhood's land?

There was woman's fearless eye,
  Lit by her deep love's truth;
There was manhood's brow, serenely high,
  And the fiery heart of youth.

What sought they thus afar?
  Bright jewels of the mine?
The wealth of seas, the spoils of war?
  They sought a faith's pure shrine!

Aye, call it holy ground,
   The soil where first they trod!
They have left unstained what there they
      found—
   Freedom to worship God!

Felicia Hemans

THE PILGRIM FATHERS

*T*HE Pilgrim Fathers,—where are they?
   The waves that brought them o'er
Still roll in the bay, and throw their spray
   As they break along the shore;
Still roll in the bay, as they rolled that day
   When the Mayflower moored below;
When the sea around was black with storms,
   And white the shore with snow.

The mists that wrapped the Pilgrim's sleep
   Still brood upon the tide;
And his rocks yet keep their watch by the deep
   To stay its waves of pride.
But the snow-white sail that he gave to the gale,
   When the heavens looked dark, is gone,—
As an angel's wing through an opening cloud
   Is seen, and then withdrawn.

[271]

The Pilgrim Fathers

The pilgrim exile,—sainted name!
  The hill whose icy brow
Rejoiced, when he came, in the morning's flame,
  In the morning's flame burns now.
And the moon's cold light, as it lay that night
  On the hillside and the sea,
Still lies where he laid his houseless head,—
  But the Pilgrim! where is he?

The Pilgrim Fathers are at rest:
  When summer's throned on high,
And the world's warm breast is in verdure drest,
  Go, stand on the hill where they lie.
The earliest ray of the golden day
  On that hallowed spot is cast;
And the evening sun as he leaves the world
  Looks kindly on that spot last.

The Pilgrim spirit has not fled:
  It walks in noon's broad light;
And it watches the bed of the glorious dead,
  With the holy stars by night.
It watches the bed of the brave who have bled,
  And still guard this ice-bound shore,
Till the waves of the bay, where the Mayflower
    lay,
  Shall foam and freeze no more.

John Pierpont

SOMETHING TO BE THANKFUL FOR

I'M glad that I am not to-day
   A chicken or a goose,
Or any other sort of bird
   That is of any use.

I'd rather be a little girl,
   Although 'tis very true,
The things I do not like at all,
   I'm often made to do.

I'd rather eat some turkey than
   To be one, thick and fat,
And so, with all my heart, to-day
   I'll thankful be for that.

                    Clara J. Denton

THANKSGIVING DAY

*O*VER the river and through the woods,
      To grandfather's house we go:
The horse knows the way
To carry the sleigh

Through the white and drifted snow.
Over the river and through the wood—
　　Oh, how the wind does blow!
　　　　It stings the toes
　　　　And bites the nose,
　　As over the ground we go.

Over the river and through the wood,
　　To have a first-rate play.
　　　　Hear the bells ring,
　　　　"Ting-a-ling-ding!"
　　Hurrah for Thanksgiving Day!
Over the river and through the wood,
　　Trot fast, my dapple-gray!
　　　　Spring over the ground,
　　　　Like a hunting hound!
　　For this is Thanksgiving Day.

Over the river and through the wood,
　　And straight through the barnyard gate.
　　　　We seem to go
　　　　Extremely slow,—
　　It is so hard to wait!
Over the river and through the wood--
　　Now grandmother's cap I spy!

Thanksgiving Day

Hurrah for the fun!
Is the pudding done?
Hurrah for the pumpkin-pie!

Lydia Maria Child

THANKSGIVING DAY

*W*ITH steadfast and unwavering faith, with
hard and patient toil,
The Pilgrims wrung their harvest from a strange
and sterile soil.
And when the leaves turned red and gold be·
neath the autumn sun,
They knelt beside the scanty sheaves their labor·
ing hands had won,
And each grave elder, in his turn, with bowed
and reverent head,
Gave thanks to bounteous Heaven for the mir·
acle of bread.

And so was born Thanksgiving Day.   That
little dauntless band,
Beset by deadly perils in a wild and alien land,
With hearts that held no fear of death, with
stern, unbending wills,

[275]

And faith as firmly founded as the grim New
    England hills,
Though pitiful the yield that sprang from that
    unfruitful sod,
Remembered in their harvest time the goodly
    grace of God.

God grant us grace to look on this, our glorious
    native land,
As but another princely gift from His almighty
    hand.
May we prove worthy of His trust and keep its
    every shore
Protected from the murderous hordes that bear
    the torch of war,
And be the future bright or dark God grant we
    never may
Forget the reverent spirit of that first Thanks-
    giving Day.

J. J. Montague

A THANKSGIVING FABLE

*I*T was a hungry pussy cat, upon Thanks-
    giving morn,
And she watched a thankful little mouse, that
    ate an ear of corn.

"If I ate that little mouse, how thankful he
    should be,
When he has made a meal himself, to make a
    meal for me;
Then with his thanks for having fed, and his
    thanks for feeding me,
With all HIS thankfulness inside, how thank-
    ful I shall be!"
Thus mused the hungry pussy cat, upon Thanks-
    giving Day;
But the little mouse had overheard and de-
    clined (with thanks) to stay.

Oliver Herford

THANKSGIVING NIGHT

*L*AST night I got to thinking, when I couldn't
    go to sleep,
Of the way Thanksgiving served me in the days
    when joy was cheap—
Of how we'd have a turkey, and of how I'd beg
    a taste
Whenever they would open up the oven door
    to "baste"

[277]

The bulging breast, and how then from the oven
    came a drift
Of tantalizing odor, such as only boys have
    sniffed.

I got to thinking of it—for I couldn't go to
    sleep—
Of mince pies in the pantry, where I'd sidle in
    and peep,
And jelly and plum butter, and the peach pre‑
    serves and cake—
And then I got to thinking of how fine 'twould
    be to take
A trip back to the old days, when the dancing
    candle light
Played pranks with all the shadows on the wall,
    Thanksgiving night.

The boys I used to play with! I could shut
    my eyes and see
The whole troop of them waiting and a-waving
    hands to me;
All freckled, ragged trousered, with their scarfs
    and mittens, too,
They made a splendid picture—but the picture
    wasn't true;

We Thank Thee

For they've grown up, as I have, and strange
    paths have lured our feet—
The paths that find To-morrow, and that never,
    never meet.

I wondered if they also were not lying half awake
And thinking of the turkey, and the jelly, and
    the cake;
And if they had their fancies of the lazy little
    street
That leads beneath the maples where the top-
    most branches meet—
And suddenly I heard them—heard the mur
    murs low and clear,
That told me they were with me, and were very,
    very near.

                   Wilbur D. Nesbit

WE THANK THEE

FOR flowers that bloom about our feet;
    For tender grass, so fresh, so sweet;
For song of bird, and hum of bee;
For all things fair we hear or see,
    Father in heaven, we thank Thee.

[279]

We Thank Thee

For blue of stream and blue of sky;
For pleasant shade of branches high;
For fragrant air and cooling breeze;
For beauty of the blooming trees,
    Father in heaven, we thank Thee.

Ralph Waldo Emerson

WE THANK THEE

*F*OR flowers so beautiful and sweet,
    For friends and clothes and food to eat,
For precious hours, for work and play,
We thank Thee this Thanksgiving Day.

For father's care and mother's love,
For the blue sky and clouds above,
For springtime and autumn gay
We thank Thee this Thanksgiving Day!

For all Thy gifts so good and fair,
Bestowed so freely everywhere,
Give us grateful hearts we pray,
To thank Thee this Thanksgiving Day.

Mattie M. Renwick

CHRISTMAS

CHRISTMAS BELLS

*A*RE you waking?" shout the breezes
 To the tree-tops waving high,
"Don't you hear the happy tidings
 Whispered to the earth and sky?
Have you caught them in your dreaming,
 Brook and rill in snowy dells?
Do you know the joy we bring you
 In the merry Christmas bells?
  Ding, dong! ding, dong, Christmas bells!

"Are you waking, flowers that slumber
 In the deep and frosty ground?
Do you hear what we are breathing
 To the listening world around?
For we bear the sweetest story
 That the glad year ever tells:
How He loved the little children,—
 He who brought the Christmas bells!
  Ding, dong! ding, dong, Christmas bells!"

George Cooper

CHRISTMAS BELLS

I HEARD the bells on Christmas Day
   Their old, familiar carols play,
     And wild and sweet
     The words repeat
Of peace on earth, good-will to men!

And thought how, as the day had come,
The belfries of all Christendom
     Had rolled along
     The unbroken song
Of peace on earth, good-will to men!

Till, ringing, swinging on its way,
The world revolved from night to day
     A voice, a chime,
     A chant sublime
Of peace on earth, good-will to men!

Then from each black, accursed mouth
The cannon thundered in the South
     And with the sound
     The carols drowned
Of peace on earth, good-will to men!

Christmas Carol

It was as if an earthquake rent
The hearth-stones of a continent,
    And made forlorn
    The households born
Of peace on earth, good-will to men!"

And in despair I bowed my head;
"There is no peace on earth," I said;
    "For hate is strong
    And mocks the song
Of peace on earth, good-will to men!"

Then pealed the bells more loud and deep:
"God is not dead; nor doth He sleep!
    The Wrong shall fail,
    The Right prevail,
With peace on earth, good-will to men!"

Henry Wadsworth Longfellow

CHRISTMAS CAROL

*T*HE earth has grown old with its burden of
    care,
But at Christmas it always is young,
The heart of the jewel burns lustrous and fair,

[285]

Christmas Carol

And its soul full of music bursts forth on the air,
  When the song of the angels is sung.

It is coming, Old Earth, it is coming to-night!
  On the snowflakes which cover thy sod
The feet of the Christ-child fall gentle and white
And the voice of the Christ-child tells out with
      delight
    That mankind are the children of God.

On the sad and the lowly, the wretched and poor,
  The voice of the Christ-child shall fall;
And to every blind wanderer open the door
Of hope that he dared not to dream of before,
  With a sunshine of welcome for all.

'The feet of the humblest may walk in the field
  Where the feet of the Holiest trod,
'This, then, is the marvel to mortals revealed
When the silvery trumpets of Christmas have
      pealed,
    That mankind are the children of God.

Phillips Brooks

A CHRISTMAS CAROL

There's a song in the air!
There's a star in the sky!
There's a mother's deep prayer
And a baby's low cry!
And the star rains its fire while the Beautiful
     sing,
For the manger of Bethlehem cradles a king.

There's a tumult of joy
O'er the wonderful birth,
For the virgin's sweet boy
Is the Lord of the earth,
Ay! the star rains its fire and the Beautiful sing,
For the manger of Bethlehem cradles a king.

In the light of that star
Lie the ages impearled;
And that song from afar
Has swept over the world,
Every home is aflame, and the Beautiful sing
In the homes of the nations that Jesus is King.

We rejoice in the light
And we echo the song
That comes down through the night

[287]

From the heavenly throng,
Ay! we shout to the lovely evangel they bring,
And we greet in his cradle our Savior and King!

Josiah Gilbert Holland

CHRISTMAS CAROL

*A*S Joseph was a-walking,
    He heard an angel sing,
"This night shall be the birthnight
    Of Christ our heavenly King.

His birth bed shall be neither
    In house nor in hall,
Nor in the place of Paradise
    But in the oxen's stall.

He neither shall be rocked
    In silver nor in gold,
But in the wooden manger
    That lieth in the mold.

He neither shall be washen
    With white wine nor with red,
But with the fair spring water
    That on you shall be shed.

[288]

Christmas Song

He neither shall be clothèd,
  In purple nor in pall,
But in the fair white linen
  That usen babies all."

As Joseph was a-walking,
  Thus did the angel sing,
And Mary's Son at midnight,
  Was born to be our King.

Then be you glad, good people;
  At this time of the year;
And light you up your candles
  For His star it shineth clear.

Unknown

CHRISTMAS SONG

*W*HY do bells for Christmas ring?
  Why do little children sing?

Once a lovely, shining star,
Seen by shepherds from afar,
Gently moved until its light
Made a manger-cradle bright.

Cradle Hymn

There a darling baby lay
Pillowed soft upon the hay.
And his mother sang and smiled,
"This is Christ, the holy child."

So the bells for Christmas ring,
So the little children sing.

Lydia Avery Coonley Ward

CRADLE HYMN

*A*WAY in a manger, no crib for a bed,
  The little Lord Jesus laid down his sweet
head.
The stars in the bright sky looked down where
  he lay—
The little Lord Jesus asleep on the hay.

The cattle are lowing, the baby awakes,
But little Lord Jesus, no crying he makes.
I love thee, Lord Jesus! look down from the sky,
And stay by my cradle till morning is nigh.

Martin Luther

EVERYWHERE, EVERYWHERE CHRIST-MAS TO–NIGHT

*C*HRISTMAS in lands of the fir tree and pine,
Christmas in lands of the palm tree and
vine;
Christmas where snow peaks stand solemn and
white,
Christmas where cornfields lie sunny and bright;
Everywhere, everywhere Christmas to-night!

Christmas where children are hopeful and gay,
Christmas where old men are patient and gray;
Christmas where peace, like a dove in its flight;
Broods o'er brave men in the thick of the fight;
Everywhere, everywhere Christmas to-night!

For the Christ child who comes is the Master
of all;
No palace too great—no cottage too small.
The angels who welcome Him sing from the
height,
"In the city of David, a King in His might."
Everywhere, everywhere Christmas to-night!

Then let every heart keep its Christmas within
Christ's pity for sorrow, Christ's hatred of sin,
Christ's care for the weakest, Christ's courage
    for right,
Christ's dread of the darkness, Christ's love of
    the light,
    Everywhere, everywhere Christmas to-night!

So the stars of the midnight which compass us
    round,
Shall see a strange glory and hear a sweet sound,
And cry, "Look! the earth is aflame with delight,
O sons of the morning rejoice at the sight."
    Everywhere, everywhere Christmas to-night!

Phillips Brooks

THE FIRST CHRISTMAS

*H*ANG up the baby's stocking;
    Be sure you don't forget—
The dear little dimpled darling!
She ne'er saw Christmas yet;
But I've told her all about it,
And she opened her big blue eyes,
And I'm sure she understood it,
She looked so funny and wise.

The First Christmas

Dear! what a tiny stocking!
It doesn't take much to hold
Such little pink toes as baby's
Away from the frost and cold.
But then, for the baby's Christmas
It will never do at all;
Why, Santa wouldn't be looking
For anything half so small.

I know what will do for the baby,
I've thought of the very best plan—
I'll borrow a stocking of grandma,
The longest that ever I can;
And you'll hang it by mine, dear mother,
Right here in the corner, so!
And write a letter to Santa,
And fasten it on to the toe.

Write, "This is the baby's stocking
That hangs in the corner here;
You never have seen her, Santa,
For she only came this year;
But she's just the blessedest baby—
And now, before you go,
Just cram her stocking with goodies,
From the top clean down to the toe."

Anonymous

[293]

GOD REST YE, MERRY GENTLEMEN

 G OD rest ye, merry gentlemen; let nothing
    you dismay,
For Jesus Christ, our Saviour, was born on
    Christmas-day.
The dawn rose red o'er Bethlehem, the stars
    shone through the gray,
When Jesus Christ, our Saviour, was born on
    Christmas-day.

God rest ye, little children; let nothing you
    affright,
For Jesus Christ, your Saviour, was born this
    happy night;
Along the hills of Galilee the white flocks sleep-
    ing lay,
When Christ, the child of Nazareth, was born
    on Christmas-day.

God rest ye, all good Christians; upon this
    blessed morn,
The Lord of all good Christians was of a woman
    born;
Now all your sorrows He doth heal, your sins
    He takes away;

For Jesus Christ, our Saviour, was born on
Christmas-day.

Dinah Maria Mulock

I SAW THREE SHIPS

I SAW three ships come sailing in,
   On Christmas day, on Christmas day;
I saw three ships come sailing in,
   On Christmas day in the morning.

Pray whither sailed those ships all three
   On Christmas day, on Christmas day?
Pray whither sailed those ships all three
   On Christmas day in the morning?

Oh, they sailed into Bethlehem
   On Christmas day, on Christmas day;
Oh, they sailed into Bethlehem
   On Christmas day in the morning.

And all the bells on earth shall ring
   On Christmas day, on Christmas day;
And all the bells on earth shall ring
   On Christmas day in the morning.

And all the angels in heaven shall sing
  On Christmas day, on Christmas day;
And all the angels in heaven shall sing
  On Christmas day in the morning.

And all the souls on earth shall sing
  On Christmas day, on Christmas day;
And all the souls on earth shall sing
  On Christmas day in the morning.

Old Carol

IF I WERE SANTA'S LITTLE BOY

IF I were Santa's little boy
  If there's a family
Of Santa Clauses in the sky
Or where their home may be,
If I were Santa's oldest son
(I only hope he has one!)
And my papa should say to me,
"What Christmas present, son, would be
The very thing you'd like to see
Within your stocking Christmas Day?"
I wouldn't stop to think (would you?)
But say,
"I want to drive the sleigh!"

If I Were Santa's Little Boy

And then when Christmas Week had come,
At nearly dawn on Christmas Day,
I'd load the sleigh with doll and drum;
And find where the reindeer were tied
And hitch them quickly up,
And I'd shout very loudly
"Clear the way!"

And crack the whip and drive the sleigh
Down from the Pole and past the clang
Of loud icicles in a row,
Blown by the wind, to where the gang
Lives, in our street,
And then I'd shout
While frightened heads of boys stuck out
From opened windows, in surprise,
With tousled hair and sleepy eyes,
I'd shout out loudly so that they
Could hear each single word I'd say.
"Hey, Dasher, Dancer!
Faster, Prancer!
Run as hard now as you can, sir!
Stop your balking
When I'm talking!
We must fill each Christmas stocking
In a hundred million places!

Dasher, Dancer, mind your paces!
Don't you dare to break the traces!"
Then I'd shake the reins and shout,
To milkmen that might be about,
"Clear the way for Santa's sleigh
Because I'm driving it today."

Mary Carolyn Davies

JEST 'FORE CHRISTMAS

*F*ATHER calls me William, sister calls me
    Will,
Mother calls me Willie, but the fellers call me
    Bill!
Mighty glad I ain't a girl—ruther be a boy,
Without them sashes, curls, an' things that's
    worn by Fauntleroy!
Love to chawnk green apples an' go swimmin'
    in the lake—
Hate to take the castor-ile they give for belly
    ache!
'Most all the time, the whole year round, there
    ain't no flies on me,
But jest 'fore Christmas I'm as good as I kin be!

[298]

Got a yeller dog named Sport, sic him on the
  cat;
First thing she knows she doesn't know where
  she is at;
Got a clipper sled, an' when us kids goes out
  to slide,
'Long comes the grocery cart, an' we all hook
  a ride!
But sometimes when the grocery man is worrited
  an' cross,
He reaches at us with his whip, an' larrups up
  his hoss,
An' then I laff an' holler, "Oh, ye never teched
  me!"
But jest 'fore Christmas I'm as good as I kin be!

Gran'ma says she hopes that when I git to be a
  man,
I'll be a missionarer like her oldest brother, Dan,
As was et up by the cannibuls that lives in Cey-
  lon's Isle,
Where every prospeck pleases, an' only man is
  vile!
But gran'ma she has never been to see a Wild
  West Show,

Nor read the life of Daniel Boone, or else I guess
she'd know

That Buff'lo Bill and cowboys is good enough
for me!

Excep' jest 'fore Christmas, when I'm good as
I kin be!

And then old Sport he hangs around, so solemn-
like an' still,

His eyes they keep a-sayin': "What's the matter, little Bill?"

The old cat sneaks down off her perch an' won-
ders what's become

Of them two enemies of hern that used to make
things hum!

But I am so perlite an' 'tend so earnestly to biz,

That mother says to father: "How improved
our Willie is!"

But father, havin' been a boy hisself, suspicions
me

When, jest 'fore Christmas, I'm as good as I
kin be!

For Christmas, with its lots an' lots of candies,
cakes, an' toys,

[300]

Was made, they say, for proper kids an' not for
   naughty boys;
So wash yer face an' bresh yer hair, an' mind yer
   p's and q's,
An' don't bust out yer pantaloons, an' don't wear
   out yer shoes;
Say "Yessum" to the ladies, an' "Yessur" to
   the men,
An' when they's company, don't pass yer plate
   for pie again;
But, thinkin' of the things yer'd like to see upon
   that tree,
Jest 'fore Christmas be as good as yer kin be!

Eugene Field

LEFT OUT

*I*F shoemakers' children are left with feet bare
I've wondered and wondered (I don't think
   it's fair)
If maybe at Christmas there aren't any toys
Left over for Santa Claus' own girls and boys!

Mary Carolyn Davies

O LITTLE TOWN OF BETHLEHEM

O LITTLE town of Bethlehem,
   How still we see thee lie!
Above thy deep and dreamless sleep
   The silent stars go by;
Yet in thy dark streets shineth
   The everlasting Light;
The hopes and fears of all the years
   Are met in thee to-night.

For Christ is born of Mary,
   And, gathered all above,
While mortals sleep, the angels keep
   Their watch of wondering love.
O morning stars, together
Proclaim the holy birth!
And praises sing to God the King,
   And peace to men on earth.

How silently, how silently,
   The wondrous gift is given!
So God imparts to human hearts
   The blessings of His heaven.

No ear may hear His coming,
    But in this world of sin,
Where meek souls will receive Him still,
    The dear Christ enters in.

O holy Child of Bethlehem,
    Descend to us, we pray;
Cast out our sin, and enter in,
    Be born in us to-day.
We hear the Christmas angels
    The great glad tidings tell;
Oh, come to us, abide with us,
    Our Lord Emmanuel!

Phillips Brooks

AN OFFERTORY

*O*H, the beauty of the Christ Child,
    The gentleness, the grace,
The smiling, loving tenderness,
    The infantile embrace!
All babyhood he holdeth,
All motherhood enfoldeth—
    Yet who hath seen his face?

Oh, the nearness of the Christ Child,
　When, for a sacred space,
He nestles in our very homes—
　Light of the human race!
We know Him and we love Him,
No man to us need prove Him—
　Yet who hath seen his face?

Mary Mapes Dodge

SANTA CLAUS

*H*E comes in the night!　He comes in the
　　night!
　He softly, silently comes;
While the little brown heads on the pillows so
　　white
　Are dreaming of bugles and drums.
He cuts through the snow like a ship through
　　the foam,
　While the white flakes around him whirl;
Who tells him I know not, but he findeth the
　　home
　Of each good little boy and girl.

Santa Claus

His sleigh it is long, and deep, and wide;
    It will carry a host of things,
While dozens of drums hang over the side,
    With the sticks sticking under the strings.
And yet not the sound of a drum is heard,
    Not a bugle blast is blown,
As he mounts to the chimney-top like a bird,
    And drops to the hearth like a stone.

The little red stockings he silently fills,
    Till the stockings will hold no more;
The bright little sleds for the great snow hills
    Are quickly set down on the floor.
Then Santa Claus mounts to the roof like a
       bird,
    And glides to his seat in the sleigh;
Not a sound of a bugle or drum is heard
    As he noiselessly gallops away.

He rides to the East, and he rides to the West,
    Of his goodies he touches not one;
He eateth the crumbs of the Christmas feast
    When the dear little folks are done.
Old Santa Claus doeth all that he can;

This beautiful mission is his;
Then, children be good to the little old man,
When you find who the little man is.

Unknown

STAR OF THE EAST

$\mathcal{S}$TAR of the East, that long ago
  Brought wise men on their way
Where, angels singing to and fro,
The Child of Bethlehem lay—
Above that Syrian hill afar
Thou shinest out to-night, O Star!

Star of the East, the night were drear
But for the tender grace
That with thy glory comes to cheer,
Earth's loneliest, darkest place,
For by that charity we see
Where there is hope for all and me.

Star of the East! show us the way
In wisdom undefiled
To seek that manger out and lay
Our gifts before the Child—

To bring our hearts and offer them
Unto our King in Bethlehem.

Eugene Field

THE STARS

*T*HE stars are lighted candles
    Upon a Christmas tree
(The branches that they hang upon
    We cannot ever see)
On Christmas Eve the angels stand
    About it after tea,
And if an angel's very good
He gets a present, as he should.

Mary Carolyn Davies

A VISIT FROM ST. NICHOLAS

*T*WAS the night before Christmas, when all
    through the house
Not a creature was stirring, not even a mouse;
The stockings were hung by the chimney with
    care,
In hopes that St. Nicholas soon would be there;
The children were nestled all snug in their
    beds,

[307]

While visions of sugar-plums danced through
their heads;
And mamma in her kerchief, and I in my cap,
Had just settled our brains for a long winter's
nap,—
When out on the lawn there arose such a
clatter,
I sprang from my bed to see what was the
matter.
Away to the window I flew like a flash,
Tore open the shutters and threw up the sash.
The moon, on the breast of the new-fallen
snow,
Gave a lustre of midday to objects below;
When what to my wondering eyes should
appear,
But a miniature sleigh and eight tiny reindeer,
With a little old driver, so lively and quick
I knew in a moment it must be St. Nick.
More rapid than eagles his coursers they came,
And he whistled and shouted and called them
by name:
"Now, Dasher! now, Dancer! now, Prancer
and Vixen!
On, Comet! on, Cupid! on, Donder and Blit-
zen!

A Visit from St. Nicholas

To the top of the porch, to the top of the wall!
Now, dash away, dash away, dash away all!"
As dry leaves that before the wild hurricane
  fly,
When they meet with an obstacle, mount to
  the sky,
So, up to the house-top the coursers they flew,
With a sleigh full of toys,—and St. Nicholas
  too.
And then in a twinkling I heard on the roof
The prancing and pawing of each little hoof.
As I drew in my head and was turning around,
Down the chimney St. Nicholas came with a
  bound.
He was dressed all in fur from his head to his
  foot,
And his clothes were all tarnished with ashes
  and soot;
A bundle of toys he had flung on his back,
And he looked like a peddler just opening his
  pack.
His eyes how they twinkled! his dimples how
  merry!
His cheeks were like roses, his nose like a
  cherry;

His droll little mouth was drawn up like a
  bow,
And the beard on his chin was as white as the
  snow.
The stump of a pipe he held tight in his teeth,
And the smoke it encircled his head like a
  wreath.
He had a broad face, and a little round belly
That shook, when he laughed, like a bowl full
  of jelly.
He was chubby and plump,—a right jolly old
  elf—
And I laughed when I saw him, in spite of
  myself.
A wink of his eye and a twist of his head
Soon gave me to know I had nothing to dread.
He spoke not a word, but went straight to his
  work,
And filled all the stockings; then turned with
  a jerk,
And laying his finger aside of his nose,
And giving a nod, up the chimney he rose.
He sprang to his sleigh, to his team gave a
  whistle,

And away they all flew like the down of a
   thistle;
But I heard him exclaim, ere he drove out of
   sight:
"Happy Christmas to all, and to all a good-
   night!"

Clement C. Moore

THE WAITS

*A*T the break of Christmas Day,
      Through the frosty starlight ringing,
Faint and sweet and far away,
   Comes the sound of children, singing,
      Chanting, singing,
         "Cease to mourn,
         For Christ is born,
      Peace and joy to all men bringing!"

Careless that the chill winds blow,
   Growing stronger, sweeter, clearer,
Noiseless footfalls in the snow
   Bring the happy voices nearer;
      Hear them singing,
         "Winter's drear,
         But Christ is here,
      Mirth and gladness with Him bringing!"

[311]

"Merry Christmas!" hear them say,
　　As the East is growing lighter;
"May the joy of Christmas Day
　　Make your whole year gladder, brighter!"
　　　　Join their singing,
　　　　　"To each home
　　　　　Our Christ has come,
　　　All Love's treasures with Him bringing!"

Margaret Deland

WHILE SHEPHERDS WATCHED THEIR FLOCKS BY NIGHT

*W*HILE shepherds watched their flocks by
　　　night,
　　All seated on the ground,
The angel of the Lord came down,
　　And glory shone around.

"Fear not," said he, for mighty dread
　　Had seized their troubled mind;
"Glad tidings of great joy I bring
　　To you and all mankind.

"To you, in David's town, this day
    Is born, of David's line,
  The Saviour, who is Christ the Lord,
    And this shall be the sign:

"The heavenly babe you there shall find
    To human view displayed,
  All meanly wrapped in swaddling bands,
    And in a manger laid."

Thus spake the seraph; and forthwith
    Appeared a shining throng
  Of angels, praising God, who thus
    Addressed their joyful song:

"All glory be to God on high,
    And to the earth be peace;
  Good will henceforth from Heaven to men
    Begin and never cease."

Nahum Tate

ÍNDEX

INDEX BY TITLES

[317]

Index by Titles

[318]

⁄ Index by Titles

[319]

Index by Titles

Index by Titles

Index by Titles

Index by Titles

INDEX OF AUTHORS

[324]

Index of Authors

[325]

Index of Authors

Index of Authors

Index of Authors

[328]

Index of Authors

Index of Authors

INDEX TO FIRST LINES

[331]

Index to First Lines

Index to First Lines

Index to First Lines

[334]

Index to First Lines

Index to First Lines

Index to First Lines